LITTLE BOOK OF BIG IDEAS

Law

First published in Great Britain in 2009

A & C Black Publishers Ltd
36 Soho Square
London W1D 3QY
Tel: 020-7758 0200
Fax: 020-7758 0222
Web: www.acblack.com

Conceived and produced by
Elwin Street Limited
144 Liverpool Road
London N1 1LA
United Kingdom
www.elwinstreet.com

Designer: Thomas Keenes
Illustrators: Richard Burgess
             and Emma Farrarons

A CIP catalogue record for this book is
available from the British Library.

ISBN 978-1-408-11148-2

Printed in Singapore

LITTLE BOOK OF BIG IDEAS

Law

Robert Hockett

Contents

Founders of International Law

Renowned Trial Lawyers

Introduction

Law is one of those institutions that is at once so pervasive and so close to us that, if asked what it is, we are apt not to know how to answer. In this respect, law might be likened to mathematics. Most of us know how to count, multiply and divide, and so forth. But if somebody asks us, 'what is a number,' we might well draw a blank. Or perhaps we'll say something like, 'you know, like zero, one, two, and so on, that's what numbers are.'

In somewhat similar fashion, this book aims to convey a sense of what law is by reference to particular concrete examples. In this case, the examples comprise 50 important legal personages, some of them associated with institutions, codes, doctrines or documents at least as well known as the individuals themselves. Also included are 10 key ideas found at the core of much legal thought and action conducted over the course of the past several millennia.

The guiding hope is that, in reading this legal 'sampler' of sorts, you will come to feel at least as much broad-brush familiarity with the law, its ideas, operations, institutions and canonical figures as you might feel with arithmetic. A related hope is that you will want to learn even more.

Notwithstanding the sampler strategy adopted by most of this book, a few general observations about law can also be made with some confidence. Here, then, is a rough attempt to provide a definition of the general nature of 'what law is'.

Well before Aristotle famously observed that the human being is 'a political animal', people had come to recognise that one thing that set them apart from many other creatures was that they were social. We tend not only to live, but indeed to stand or to fall, together. And much of what we accomplish, even as individuals, we do against the backdrop of shared institutions.

Consider the 'institutions' of language or money. We often think solitarily, or purchase and sell alone. Yet each of us is able to do these things precisely by dint of the ease of articulating or transacting – made possible because of shared vocabulary and legal tender. Structures and institutions of these sorts are all, in one sense or another, 'laws'. Some of these patterns or structures are laws only in the 'spontaneous regularity' sense: they are widely observed conventions, such as the way by which we register assent with the word 'yes'.

A sociologist or linguist visiting from another society might say that those who follow these conventions tend, 'as a rule', or 'in lawlike fashion', to act in these ways. And of course in the same way, we sometimes talk of 'laws of nature', in referring to similar regularities in the movements of physical objects and some nonhuman animals.

What sets 'the law' in the courtroom or legislative sense apart from these cases is, perhaps, simply this: the laws promulgated and enforced through political authority are regularities *deliberately chosen*. We don't merely happen into patterns of this sort. We design and enact and enforce them.

This renders law of the designed, enacted and enforced sort potentially a great blessing, and a great curse. For it offers the opportunity to *decide* the patterns and regularities by which we interact with one another. And thus it offers the prospect of patterning our interactions wisely, sensibly, justly – in ways that better our lives as individuals, as family members, as parties to all manner of transactions, and ultimately, as citizens.

One way of looking at all of the personages, codes, institutions and ideas discussed here, then, is as contributors and contributions to the combined effort to arrange society sensibly, and justly, in a manner enabling each of us to lead lives well lived.

Hammurabi

Hammurabi was the sixth king of the ancient Mesopotamian city of Babylon and first emperor of what became the Babylonian Empire. With Babylon being the focus of recorded history from this period, he will long be known for his public works and his military conquests. It is primarily for his early law code, however, that he figures in legal conversation and iconography today.

Born: 1795 BCE, Babylon
Importance: introduced first publicly accessible code of law.
Died: 1750 BCE, Babylon

Hammurabi inherited the Babylonian throne in 1792 BCE from his father, the First Dynasty king, Sin-muballit. At the time, Babylon was one of a number of powerful city-states in Mesopotamia (present day Iraq), many of which frequently fought for control of the fertile Tigris and Euphrates plains. Culturally, Babylon was the most influential of these principalities and had achieved political domination over a number of others, even before Hammurabi's time.

In his first decades as king, Hammurabi took advantage of a peaceful period in the region to instigate and oversee many important projects for public works. These included the expansion of the city temples, fortification of the city's defensive walls, improving its calendar in the light of astronomical recordings, and managing the flood plains and vast herds of cattle under Babylonian control. A number of successful wars from 1766 BCE and 1750 BCE – against the kingdoms of Elam, Larsa and Mari among others – resulted in Babylon gaining uncontested

'If a man destroys the eye of another man, they shall destroy his eye.'

Code of Law

dominion over most of Mesopotamia. Hammurabi ruled in peace for another decade, until his death in 1750 BCE.

In addition to his public works, Hammurabi's chief legacy lies in the new code of law that he promulgated for Babylon early in his reign. The celebrated 'Code of Hammurabi' is perhaps most widely known today for its *lex talionis* (law of revenge) provision: 'an eye for an eye, a tooth for a tooth.' Etched onto 12 stone stelae in Akkadian, the vernacular language of Babylon, these were placed in the city centre so that all – at least those who were literate – could read them. (Their remnants are now at the Louvre in Paris.) This form of publication set a precedent for later conceptions of codification and rule of law (see pages 19 and 20; see also Lon Fuller, page 92). It also suggested the immutability of an earthly ruler's capacity to change it. This was reinforced by an inscription above the code, to the effect that Hammurabi had received the law from the sun deity, Shamash. This claim is viewed as an early statement of 'higher law' authority, possibly setting a precedent for later conceptions of natural law and natural rights (see pages 62 and 124).

Exculpatory evidence: Evidence that is favourable to the defendant in a criminal trial, with the potential to clear the defendant of guilt. Inculpatory evidence is used to prove the defendant's guilt.

Although the 282 provisions of the Code of Hammurabi were largely devoted to criminal matters and punishments (compare the Qing Code, page 30), it also included a number of more 'progressive' elements that have endured in most modern legal codes. Among these are both the principle of presumption of evidence and the right of the accused to proffer exculpatory evidence.

Owing to Hammurabi's significance as an early codifier and lawgiver, his image is found in much civic art and architecture to this day.

Constitutionalism and Rule of Law

Among those ideas thought distinctive of modern ideals of good governance is that of the 'rule of law', or a 'government of laws, not men'. The essence of the idea is that the law is a system of principles or rules to which all individuals – including those who govern – are subject. Even the sovereign is subject to the constraints of the law, as distinguished from arbitrary personal preference or whim.

Although it is only in comparatively modern times that this idea has secured broad global purchase in the form of what has increasingly come to be called 'constitutionalism', the ideal is actually of venerable vintage. It appears to originate in the notion of 'higher', or 'natural', laws or patterns to which all actions and events are in one or another sense bound (see Natural law and Natural rights and bills of rights, pages 62 and 124).

In classical Greek thought, this idea is found in the concept of 'Logos', from which our word 'logic' and the suffix '-logy' derive. In this, and in other cases, thinkers have suggested that actions – including governmental actions – at variance with the proper or natural 'way' of things are either ethically wrongful, apt to result in disharmony and ill fortune, or both.

Through Stoic thought, the idea of the Logos found its way into Roman philosophy and law, ultimately manifesting itself, along with counterpart Hebraic traditions of God's Torah, in the European natural law tradition. In somewhat similar fashion, the rough Chinese counterpart known as the Tao seems to have found its way into East Asian legal thought through the socially oriented counterpart notion of Li, or social propriety, which figures prominently in Confucian traditions that have been influential in East Asian societies. The comparable Indian concept of dharma, for its part, proceeded directly in Indian thought from a notion of cosmic order to a notion of social order. (The wheel, long a symbol of dharma in Indian iconography, is found on the Indian flag to this day.) In all of these cases, the crucial notion was that even political rulers and their decrees were themselves considered, in one or another sense, subject to the 'higher' law in question.

What distinguishes the modern conception of rule of law is perhaps less the idea of political sovereign-transcending authority itself, than the commitment to a form of legal *redress* that nongovernmental persons might have against law-violating officials. In this sense, the ideals of constitutionalism and rule of law are intimately connected not only with the philosophic concept of natural law, but also with the institutional notions of separation of powers and judicial review (see page 36).

The idea of earthly non-sovereigns (in this case clerics) rather than Heaven alone holding sovereigns personally accountable in the name of higher law has precedents of course. Examples include the biblically recorded practice of the anointing of King Saul by the prophet Samuel; medieval European pontiffs' authority both to coronate and excommunicate European monarchs; and the Chinese Confucian notion of 'zhengming', by which unjust rulers are considered to be false rulers and subject to dethronement by sages. But it seems to be in the Magna Carta that we first find a practice whereby noneccelsial personages hold a monarch accountable to polity-constitutive law – in this case, the nobles versus King John of England (see page 26).

Moses

Moses is doubtless the best known of the ancient lawgivers in the Western tradition. Images of the white-bearded, long-haired prophet, holding stone tablets bearing the Ten Commandments over his head, are a staple of moral and legal iconography.

Born: early fourteenth century BCE, ancient Egypt
Importance: led ancient Israelites out of Egypt; delivered the Ten Commandments.
Died: thirteenth century BCE, ancient Palestine

According to the Bible's book of Exodus, Moses was the son of Amram, one of the Levite tribe of Israel descended from Jacob, and Amram's wife, Jochebed. His birth occurred in Egypt, for, according to the book of Genesis, Amram's father, Kohath, emigrated to Egypt with 70 of Jacob's household.

Moses was born at a time when the Egyptian Pharaoh, probably Ramesses II, had ordered all male Hebrew children drowned. According to the Exodus account, in order to save the young Moses, Jochebed first kept him hidden, then set him adrift on the river Nile in a small ark fashioned from bullrushes. Pharoah's daughter, Bithiah, then bathing in the Nile with her handmaidens, is said to have spotted the small ark and ultimately adopted the child. His actual mother, Jochebed, whose identity was unknown to Bithiah, was later employed as a nurse to Moses.

According to the biblical account, as a young man in the Egyptian royal family, Moses witnessed an Egyptian slave master beating a Hebrew slave, became enraged, and killed the slave master. Fleeing across the Sinai, he became a shepherd in Midian and married the Midianite, Zipporah.

One day while tending his flocks, according to Exodus, Moses saw a bush that was in flames but miraculously was not consumed. Investigating the strange sight, Moses was instructed by God to go back to Egypt and lead his now enslaved people to

freedom. Then came the familiar history in which, assisted by a sequence of plagues visited upon Egypt by God, Moses and his brother Aaron secured passage out of Egypt by the Israelites. There followed a period of 40 years' wandering in the wilderness before God instructed Moses to lead his followers to Canaan.

It was during the wandering period that Moses's significance as a lawgiver emerged. According to the biblical account, Moses ascended Mount Sinai to commune with God. There, God delivered to Moses what became known as the Ten Commandments, which Moses brought down to the Israelites etched upon two stone tablets. These became the core of Jewish and, subsequently, Christian, and then Islamic law.

Many of the particular injunctions included among the Ten Commandments are of course central to moral codes worldwide. The principal significance from a legal point of view, however, lies in two features in particular. First, there is the idea that the law is handed down from on high, with the lawgiver – in this case, Moses – serving the role simply of intermediary. And second, there is the idea that the law is to be publicly recorded and accessible. The first idea relates directly to the idea of natural law (see page 62), which has proved so influential to legal thinking. The second flows neatly into that of the rule of law (see page 10), which lies at the core of most modern legal systems.

Early Lawgivers and Laws

Solon

Solon is the archetypal ancient Greek figure – poet, philosopher and statesman in one. He stands as founding father to Athens, as his earlier counterpart, Lycurgus, does to Sparta. Since Athens and Sparta between them were models for generations of legal and political thinkers, this makes Solon and Lycurgus twinned early founders of Western legal and political thought.

Born: 638 BCE, Athens
Importance: legendary founder of ancient Athenian constitution.
Died: 558 BCE, Cyprus

Solon's origins are widely debated, but what seems to be largely agreed upon is this: Athens was, by Solon's adulthood, subject to much civil strife along clan and economic class lines. After decades of fighting and social dysfunction, some elders approached Solon, held in high regard for his wisdom, asking him to mediate among warring factions and enact a new set of laws for the city.

Solon's reforms were recorded in verse upon large wooden slabs erected in a publicly accessible location. Particularly noteworthy among them were provisions that all classes of citizen be represented in the *ekklesia* – Athens's legislative assembly – and that a court – called the *heliaia* – be likewise formed, to which any citizen then might have access in bringing suit against anyone accused of violating rights. These institutions are widely thought to have formed the foundation for Athenian – and hence ultimately all Western – democracy.

Solon is also credited with having enacted legal reforms aimed at eliminating common practices associated with economic distress, such as prohibiting indentured servitude for bankrupts and other forms of enslavement. Other legal reforms were directed against wealthy citizens who used their material assets to take advantage of the levers of governance.

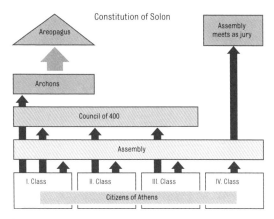

Constitution of Solon

Areopagus

Assembly meets as jury

Archons

Council of 400

Assembly

I. Class

II. Class

III. Class

IV. Class

Citizens of Athens

Above: Solon's constitution paved the way for modern democracy. It provided all citizens with political representation and judicial access and also gave citizens the power to both elect their representatives and call them to account.

Sparta, the other influential Greek city-state of this period, had its own lawgiver in the form of Lycurgus. There is little agreement over whether Lycurgus was even a historical, rather than mythic, figure, let alone when he was born. Legend has it that he was a tough and laconic war veteran, originally retained as tutor to the young Spartan king, Charialus. He then became leader in his own right, whereupon he put into place many legal reforms, known as the 'Great Rhetra'.

Lycurgus's Sparta developed into being, along with Athens, one of the two most influential Greek city-states. It also seems to have been an object of fascination to many subsequent political figures and utopian philosophers, including Plato, whose Republic was partly modelled upon it. The same holds for many Roman thinkers and later leaders of militarised states. Though these particular influences are perhaps marginal, the ideals of divided political sovereignty, rough social equality, and wealth redistribution in the interest thereof have proved more enduring.

Manu

In the Hindu tradition, Manu is said to have been the progenitor of humankind. For this reason, the world's people are called 'Manavas' in Hindu scripture. Some of these, the Brahmanas, are designated by Hindu law as those who devote themselves to the study of sacred legal and spiritual texts.

Born: between 200 BCE and 200 CE
Importance: by tradition, the giver of Hindu laws.
Died: between 200 BCE and 200 CE

Manu is said to have been a wise king, devoted to truth and virtue. According to legend, while he was washing his hands in a river, an avatar of Vishnu in the form of a fish warned him of an impending flood that would engulf the world. Manu accordingly constructed a boat, which then housed his family and various seeds and animals, all to repopulate the earth once the flood waters receded. The parallels with the Biblical story of Noah and other ancient deluge stories, notably the Mesopotamian, are striking.

According to the *Mahabharata*, the great Indian epic, Manu fathered 10 children from whom all post-diluvian people of the earth are descended. As for legal offspring, a number of important bodies of law are said to have been handed down by Manu. Among them are the *Manava Grihyasutra*, the *Manava Sulbasutra*, and the *Manava Dharmashastra*. Together, Manu's laws are known as the *Manu Smriti*. The last of those mentioned, the *Dharmashastra*, is still treated to this day as a code of

'Justice, being violated, destroys; justice, being preserved, preserves: therefore justice must not be violated, lest violated justice destroy us.'

The Laws of Manu, chapter VIII

religious life and ritual by traditional Hindus. Indeed, the very word 'dharma' corresponds to the Greek word 'Logos' and the Chinese word 'Tao', each of them words for the concept of patterned regularity, the last word, in turn, being cognate with the word 'religion' (root *religare*) itself.

Historians believe that the texts attributed to Manu date to some time in the period between 200 BCE and 200 CE. Many of the particulars of the texts have at various times been controversial. Among the reasons are that some of them apparently sanction divisions among castes, while others seemingly sanction the subjection of women.

> 213. It is the nature of women to seduce men in this (world); for that reason the wise are never unguarded in (the company of) females.
> 214. For women are able to lead astray in (this) world not only a fool, but even a learned man, and (to make) him a slave of desire and anger.
> 215. One should not sit in a lonely place with one's mother, sister, or daughter; for the senses are powerful, and master even a learned man.
> (from *Manu Smriti*, Chapter 2)

Other provisions of Manu's law codes, however, have been argued by scholars to enjoin contrary values to those of caste division and subjugation. Manu's work as a whole, moreover, has been much admired by spiritualists, vitalists and romantic philosophers for its affirmations of life. For legal purposes, however, the significance of Manu is much like that of Hammurabi, Moses, Solon and Muhammad (see pages 8, 12, 14 and 22): he stands as a great civilization's symbol of earthly law bearing superearthly provenance.

Justinian I

Justinian is probably the single most important figure in the
history of civil law (see page 20). His *Corpus Iuris* forms the core
of most systems of law now descended from the Roman tradition,
and its doctrines have crucially influenced other legal systems
including those of common law.

Born: 482, Tauresium,
Eastern Roman Empire
Importance: his codification
of the diffuse elements of
Roman law became the
basis for all subsequent civil
law legal systems and
codes.
Died: 565, Constantinople,
Eastern Roman Empire

Justinian was born Petrus Sabbatius, a peasant in the
province of Dardinia, located in what is now central
Serbia. He later took his name from his Uncle Justin,
brother of his mother, Vigilantia. Justin, who was a
member of the imperial guard, adopted his nephew
and took him to Constantinople, eastern capital of
the Roman Empire. This enabled the young Justinian
to receive an education. He is known to have studied
law, theology and Roman history.

In 518, Justin found himself emperor upon the
death of the then emperor, Anastasius, apparently
thanks in part to the maneuvering of Justinian.
During Justin's brief nine-year reign, through most of which
Justin was ailing, Justinian is thought to have functioned much as
de facto ruler. Justin named him associate emperor in 527, and
upon Justin's death that same year, Justinian became sole emperor.

Two years later, Justinian married Theodora. The pair reigned
over a period of great activity, reform and expansion of territory
on the part of the eastern Roman Empire, with Justinian
becoming known as 'the emperor who never sleeps' in view of his
prodigious energies.

Justinian is best known to lawyers for his pioneering effort to
codify the, by then, sprawling mass of Roman legal provisions.
These took the form of scattered constitutions, edicts and rules

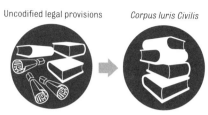

Uncodified legal provisions   *Corpus Iuris Civilis*

Above: The *Corpus Iuris Civilis* brought together a mass of legal provisions and comprised four parts. The *Codex Iustinianus* consisted of post-second-century enactments, the *Digesta* covered older legal documents, the supplemental *Novellae* comprised new provisions from Justinian's reign, and the *Institutiones* distilled the principles from the other three documents.

laid down in court decisions, among others. Systematisers in the tradition of Ulpian (see page 32) were hard-pressed to keep up with them by Justinian's day.

Justinian assigned the *Quaestor Tribonian* to oversee the work but played an active role as well. The resultant *Corpus Iuris Civilis* was a mammoth accomplishment, and one that forms the basis of all civil law systems to this day (see page 20). Its innovative attempt to gather together and impose order upon, as well as to exposit in principled fashion, the previously scattered provisions of law, set the pattern for subsequent codification movements (see page 20). In many ways, we have lived in an 'era of codes' ever since.

Justinian's influence upon continental European law has been particularly far-reaching. Roman Law doctrines and methods have formed the basis of most continental law codes and legal systems since early medieval times; and those doctrines and methods, for their parts, have stemmed principally from the writings of medieval and subsequent legal thinkers interpreting Justinian's *Corpus Iuris Civilis*. (See Bartolus, Savigny, and Jhering, pages 66, 72 and 78.) In an important sense, then, Justinian's empire was never lost. It has continued in the form of Europe's still quite Roman law.

Common Law and Civil Law, Custom and Code

As an historical distinction, the common law versus civil law dichotomy is a distinction between those legal systems descended from the British model on the one hand and those from the Roman law model on the other.

Prominent common law systems, besides the British example, are the American, Australian, Canadian, Indian, Israeli, Nigerian, Pakistani and South African legal systems. There is, unsurprisingly, a strong correspondence between members of the British Commonwealth and nations with legal systems rooted in British common law. Common law influence is also pronounced in those legal systems that have historically been associated with other former associates of the UK, such as the US.

Just as most nations with common law legal systems have historically borne close political connections (albeit not always direct and not always voluntary!) to the UK, so have most nations with civil law systems historically borne close direct or indirect political connections to the Roman Empire (again, not always voluntary). Civil law systems are accordingly encountered throughout most of continental Europe and in many nations elsewhere – for example, in some parts of Africa and much of Asia, Eastern Europe and South America.

Between the two of them, the originally British common law and originally Roman civil law form the fundaments of most modern legal systems. Many other legal systems, moreover, include significant elements of one or the other, or both, either by dint of deliberate incorporation or shared historical origin. The Scandinavian systems and certain elements of the northern

Germanic legal traditions, for example, appear to have originated as common law systems akin to that developed by the northern Europeans' British cousins.

Perhaps more interesting than the historical distinction between common law and civil law systems, is the functional or 'stylistic' distinction, although there is considerable danger of overstating this distinction today. The difference is roughly that, in civil law, legal authorities attempt to foresee and legally provide against conflicts of interest between citizens ahead of time, while in common law, judges are afforded discretion in crafting legal doctrine flexibly in response to new problems as they arise. In this sense, the common law/civil law distinction is one between law that is 'codified' *ex ante* (in advance) and law that is developed incrementally, rather like 'custom', *ex post* (after the fact).

> **Codification:** The process of collecting and restating the law of a jurisdiction in certain areas, usually by subject. The result is a legal code.

In theory, the more detailed a code, the less discretion need be afforded to judges in resolving cases pursuant to open-ended principles. In civil law systems, judges are passive appliers of pre-legislated provisions. By contrast, common law eschews the idea of providing for every conceivable legal dispute in advance. Instead judges enjoy a broader mandate to exercise discretion and prudence in 'doing justice' in accordance with broadly stated legal principles.

It must be emphasised, however, that the common law versus civil law distinction is, in modern times, no more than an ideal. No system today is clearly of one or the other variety. Common law systems, like those of the UK and US, are nowadays pervaded by detailed legislative codes. And civil law systems, like those of France and Germany, require judges at least as thoughtful as their Anglo-American peers in the interest of correct application of complex provisions.

Muhammad

Since Islam does not distinguish between religious life, political life and legal life, as the founder of a religious tradition Muhammad was the founder of a legal and political tradition as well.

Born: *c.* 570, Mecca, Arabia
Importance: prophet and founder of Islam.
Died: 632, Medina, Arabia

Muhammad was born to a distinguished Meccan family, orphaned at a young age, and subsequently raised by an uncle. In young adulthood he became a merchant and married at the age of 26. In time he grew discontented with life in Mecca and began a practice of meditation and prayer in a mountain cave. According to tradition, at about the age of 40 he was visited in his cave by the angel Gabriel, who revealed truths of God to him from that time on.

Several years after the first visitation, Muhammad began to preach his revelations publicly. He proclaimed that God is one, that full surrender – the meaning of the word 'Islam' – to God is required by God, and that he, Muhammad, was God's messenger as had been Adam, Noah, Abraham, Moses, David and Jesus.

Early in this period, few accepted Muhammad's message; he and his few followers at the time were persecuted. In consequence, they migrated to Medina in 622, at which point the Islamic calendar begins. The sundry tribes who inhabited the environs of Medina had been embroiled in violent feuding for many years and, according to tradition, they asked Muhammad to mediate among them. In time he was able to unite the tribes into one polity under ordinances that he received in the form of revelations.

Muhammad's successes in the vicinity of Medina aroused suspicions among those who had persecuted him and his

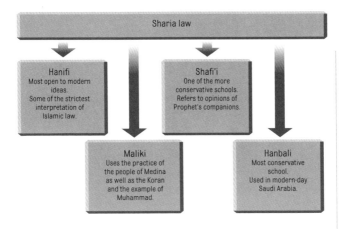

Above: Sharia law is divided into four schools: Hanifi, Maliki, Shafi'i and Hanbali. Each school has its own distinct teachings and beliefs.

followers in Mecca. In short order, conflict began to break out between the Meccans and Muhammad's followers in Medina. A series of small-scale wars ensued, by the end of which, in about 632, most of the Arabian peninsula had been conquered by Muhammad's followers and converted to Islam. In effect, it was the first Islamic state.

At the end of this period, Muhammad made a pilgrimage to Mecca and delivered what came to be known as his Farewell Speech. He left his followers with a number of final injunctions. Several months later he was afflicted with head pains and weakness and succumbed after a few days. His tomb is now housed in the Mosque of the Prophet in Medina. Sharia law in today's Islamic states derives from the written record of Muhammad's revelations, known as the Koran.

King William I and the Domesday Book

When William I – 'the Conquerer' – successfully invaded England in 1066, he wanted to know what he had gained. With characteristic Norman efficiency, he accordingly commissioned an official survey. According to the *Anglo-Saxon Chronicle*, he sent commissioners across the land to learn 'what or how much each landholder had in land and livestock, and what it was worth.'

Born: 1027, Falaise, France
Importance: oversaw first ever public register of property holdings.
Died: 1087, Rouen, France

A significant part of William's motive was, of course, to learn whom he might tax and for how much. But the project bore great collateral significance. For one thing, it served in effect as a census. For another, it served as a registry of property – a comprehensive public record of who owned land and where. Such records have proved essential, in modern states, to the maintenance of stable property regimes wherein those who own land are able to hold – and thus also to sell or bequeath – secure title.

Some scholars maintain that England's head start in developing a well-recorded, and thus enforceable, property regime of this sort enabled it in subsequent years to lead Europe in the development of a modern economy based upon free enterprise. While that seems a bit of a stretch – the Industrial Revolution did not occur until some seven centuries later – it is not entirely without basis: one of the first tasks that lawyers began to pursue upon the fall of Soviet-style governments in Eastern Europe in the early 1990s, intriguingly enough, was that of developing comprehensive registries of property holdings – late-twentieth-century Domesday Books, as it were.

Above: The Domesday Book was a comprehensive record of property held throughout Norman England following William I's conquest. During the Middle Ages, it was often referred to for evidence in legal disputes, a practice that still occurs in certain cases today.

The *Domesday Book* can now be seen on display in the museum at the National Archives, Kew, in southwest London. The name 'Domesday' derives from the Old English dom, meaning 'accounting' or 'reckoning'. It is in that sense cognate with the more popular 'doomsday' employed to refer to the Last Judgment as described in the Bible's book of Revelation. Unlike that day, however, which is an end, William I's Domesday was a beginning – the fruits of which can now be seen in every nation where property titles are publicly recorded and, in consequence, secure.

King John and the Magna Carta

Magna Carta (Latin for 'Great Charter'), portions of which remain part of the law of England and Wales to this day, is the font of the British Constitution, the American Constitution and, through them, of many other constitutions worldwide. It established the prototype both for the rule of law (see page 10) and for the separation of powers (see page 36) so characteristic of modern government today.

Born: 1167, Oxford, England
Importance: early founder of British Constitution and its descendants.
Died: 1216, Lincolnshire, England

Magna Carta was the outcome of a 'power struggle', as one might call it today, between England's King John and his nobles. It had precedent, however, in the Charter of Liberties that King Henry I had voluntarily issued in 1100. Henry had formally announced that his powers were constrained by law – an early statement in Britain of the idea of rule of law. John, however, found occasion to be somewhat more hesitant.

As a result of political intrigues in France, about 1202, French king, Philip Augustus, declared John's French lands forfeit. A series of wars on the Continent ensued, which resulted in significant military losses to John. He lost the wealthy French territory of Normandy, among other lands, and with them a principal source of revenue. Worse still, he became embroiled in a political – and impending military – confrontation with Pope Innocent III and King Philip, once more, from 1208 to 1212. John was ultimately forced to cede England and Ireland as papal territories and rent them from Innocent.

John now needed money, and he had lost his wealthiest sources of income. Acting as many governments do, he began to raise taxes. This, in addition to the disgraces wrought by his unsuccessful conflicts on the Continent, ultimately resulted in a rebellion on the part of the most powerful barons of England. They entered London in force in June 1215, with support from the city's residents. John was forced to agree to what were then called the 'Articles of the Barons', formally limiting his powers, in the meadow at Runnymede. Chancery recorded a formal document memorialising the

'To no one will we sell, to no one will we refuse or delay right or justice'
Magna Carta

agreement, and this came to be known as Magna Carta. Though the document was amended various times over the ensuing centuries, a number of its more striking provisions remain in force to this day.

Probably the best known among Magna Carta's provisions is Clause 29, the basis of 'due process' provisions found in most written constitutions today (see page 28). Clause 29 prohibits deprivation by the sovereign of any person's life, liberty or property save in consequence of guilt found at trial by a jury of one's peers. Other clauses provide for habeas corpus – the right of one held in detention by the government to challenge the detention in court with a view to vindicating his or her rights – and for the availability of courts in which to vindicate these rights. It is scarcely surprising, then, that Lord Coke (see page 34) later came to view Magna Carta as the font of British civil liberties – liberties that subsequently came to be fought for and cherished by individuals worldwide.

Trial by Jury and Due Process of Law

Along with the rule of law and judicial review (see pages 10 and 36), the institutions of trial by jury and due course of law are widely viewed, at least in the Anglophone world, as foundational guarantors of political freedom. So important are they considered, in fact, that they typically figure among those very natural rights enumerated in most modern Anglophone bills of rights (see page 124).

A jury trial is a legal proceeding in which laypersons – classically 12 – apply the law as stated by a judge to facts that emerge from courtroom examination and argumentation. In so doing, jurors find either for the complaining party (the plaintiff) or for the defending party (the defendant).

In criminal proceedings, the plaintiff in question is the state. For this reason, jury trial in criminal proceedings has been cherished as a means of limiting governments' power to deprive citizens of liberty or property. The guiding idea is that the defendant's peers serve as final arbiters over whether a fellow citizen shall be deemed criminal and punished.

In civil proceedings, of course, the latter function is not implicated. There is accordingly more scope for departure from jury trials in favor of a judicial or arbitral decision in such cases. Jury trial is nevertheless often extolled (even in civil cases) as a means by which fresh perspective and a 'folk sense of justice' can find their way into court dispositions.

The origins of trial by jury are somewhat obscure and remain subject to dispute. Because jury trial is characteristic of legal systems descended from British common law, while rare among civil law and other systems (see page 20), it is thought by many to have evolved from north and west Germanic practice. But it also is known that the Franks of mid-Continental Europe maintained customs much like those that grew into the modern jury system. The Normans who entered Britain in the eleventh century are also known to have been familiar with similar practices. Whatever the origins of juries, however, they were characteristic features of litigation in Britain from quite early on. By the thirteenth century, they were viewed as a lynchpin of 'the rights of Englishmen'. Magna Carta itself enshrined them (see page 26).

Originally, the jury served not simply as a deciding, but also as an active investigatory body. Today, the jury confines itself mainly to deliberations upon the persuasiveness of evidence offered by others, then to determining the legal significance of the facts it thus finds in light of instruction by judges as to the law. Nominally speaking, the jury is meant to find for the plaintiff or defendant strictly in accordance with the law. However, in some cases, juries occasionally exercise discretion to disregard the law itself on behalf of a defendant thought unjustly prosecuted.

So-called due process of law is perhaps best viewed as a generalisation of the cherished right of trial by jury. Insofar as the latter is seen as a guarantor of the defendant's rights as against arbitrary action by the state, it is effectively treated as a core feature of a method of adjudication that bears the same virtue. But the method in question bears other constitutive features as well. These include parties' rights to bring evidence to the attention of the court, to question the evidence brought by their adversaries, to argue the legal significance of such evidence, and even to argue the actual content of the law itself. All of these rights, which jointly constitute a robust procedural *fairness*, constitute in so doing that 'process' of law understood to be 'due' to free and equal citizens of a polity under the rule of law.

Early Lawgivers and Laws

Confucius and the Qing Code

The Qing Code, also known as the 'Great Legal Code', was the culmination of centuries of legal codification (see page 19) in imperial China – a practice that began in the early seventh century with the Tang Code. By the time of its repeal, in 1912, by the Kuomintang government, the Qing Code comprised nearly 2,000 provisions and had been in force for almost 300 years.

Born: 551 BCE, Lu, China
Importance: influenced first modern Chinese legal code.
Died: 479 BCE, Lu, China

Crucial to the content of the great Chinese law codes was the thought of Kung'-Fu-tzu, better known in the West as 'Confucius'. Confucius, whose thought has been abidingly influential in East Asian culture for centuries, was born near the city of Qufu, in the state of Lu, circa 551 BCE He lived in Lu for most of his life and died in Qufu in 479 BCE.

Notwithstanding humble origins, Confucius, apparently wholly self-taught, had developed a reputation throughout Lu for his learnedness early on in his life. His advice came to be sought by many politically powerful officials. By the age of 53, he had become Justice Minister of Lu. In that post, he was able to put directly into practice the philosophy of filial piety and mannered social propriety that he worked out over the course of his life and ultimately published in the celebrated *Analects*.

Perhaps owing to their Confucian contents, traditional Chinese legal codes were primarily directive in nature, embodying Confucian ideals of social control effectuated by a central governmental administration. The codes were in consequence criminal in flavour, delineating forms of behaviour considered to be offences and stipulating punishments to be administered upon conviction. In accordance with their Confucian purposes, the codes were viewed as instruments not only of social control, but also of moral reform of offenders.

The Qing Code was in keeping with the Chinese tradition of legal codification but more extensive and detailed than its predecessors. It was widely admired for its precision of expression and elegance of structure and was the first Chinese legal document translated into Western languages – English in 1810, French in 1812.

While formally a criminal code, the Qing Code functioned in part as a civil code as well. Private plaintiffs were able to bring complaints against defendants under the code's provisions. This availability, combined with magistrates' discretionary authority to apply code provisions flexibly and in keeping with local custom, enabled the development of a de facto law of tort under the protection of the nominally criminal Code.

When the Kuomintang came into power in 1912, the era of imperial law, strictly speaking, ended. The new republican government looked actively to European and Japanese law codes in an effort to modernise China. Intriguingly, however, much of the Qing Code remained in effect in Hong Kong (for the Chinese population, at least): as late as 1971, prior to passage of the Marriage Act, Chinese men in Hong Kong could legally engage in polygamy by dint of its allowance under the Qing Code.

While that has, of course, changed, many other norms once embodied in the Qing Code are making a comeback of sorts, as the People's Republic of China (PRC) government endeavours to recover elements of the Confucian past in industrialising China.

Law of tort: Tort law defines what constitutes a legal injury and establishes the circumstances under which one person may be held liable for another's injury. It excludes wrongs caused by breaches of trust or contract.

Ulpian

Little is known of Domitius Ulpianus except that he was evidently born in Tyre and wrote most of what he left us between the years 211 and 222. His primary significance today is that he was the first, and thus precedent-setting, in a succession of jurists who interpreted and arranged the sundry provisions of Roman law into a coherent and intelligible system of law. Roman – or 'civil' – law (see page 20) has been prized for these qualities of coherence and systematisation ever since.

Born: date unknown, Tyre, Lebanon
Importance: early exemplar of what became the long-standing Roman law tradition of synthetically interpreting and coherently systematising formerly diffuse legal provisions.
Died: 228, Rome

The first record of Ulpian in public life is his role as a member of the Council of Septimius Severus. He later became Master of the Requests under Caracalla and, later still, chief advisor and Praefectus Praetorio under Emperor Alexander. He was, alas, ultimately murdered in the palace while thus serving, during a riot involving soldiers and a mob of citizens.

Ulpian is best known to legal scholars as the author of a number of highly regarded texts. Among these are the *Ad Sabinum*, a commentary on the *ius civile* – or civil law – of Rome; the *Ad Edictum*, a commentary on the collected edicts of the emperors to date; and the *De Officio Proconsulis Libri*, an exposition of Roman criminal law. These works are prized for their clarity of expression, logic of arrangement and elegance of style.

From Ulpian onward, Roman law came to be known for its jurist-commentators, all of them cast in the Ulpianian mode. Prior to the institution of commentary of Ulpian's kind, 'the law' had been a more or less scattered affair, taking the form of sundry principles enunciated by judges deciding particular cases and ad hoc edicts delivered by various emperors. Ulpian was among the first to make a serious effort to extract basic principles from particular decisions and edicts, from which he synthesised a coherent body of systematic legal doctrine. This practice not only facilitated broad understanding and dissemination of the law as it had by that point developed, but also aided the further orderly development of the law by making patent previously latent principles, so that they could guide future decisions and enactments. Roman law has been admired as *ratio scripta* or 'written reason' – ever since, both by Continental European, and by other, lawyers and legal scholars.

> 'Justice is the constant and perpetual will to allot to every man his due.'
>
> Ulpian

Indeed, what Ulpian and his successors did for Roman law may best be appreciated in the light of relatively recent developments in British common law and its offspring until comparatively recently. Many who decried the disorderly motley that was the common law, and accordingly called for codification (see entries on common law and civil law, custom and code, and Bentham, pages 20 and 70), had the perceivably superior example of Roman law very much in view. Against that backdrop, the significance of Lords Coke, Blackstone, and Mansfield (see pages 34, 38 and 54) appear in a new light: they can be viewed as the common law's Ulpians.

Sir Edward Coke

Many people with some knowledge of legal history are aware of the importance of Sir William Blackstone (see page 38) in the development of early American law. Regrettably, fewer seem cognisant of the equally profound role of Sir Edward Coke – both in development of the modern British and, through it, the US and subsequent constitutions.

Born: 1552, Norfolk, England
Importance: influential judicial contributor to and theorist of the British Constitution.
Died: 1634, London, England

Coke received his education first at Norwich School, then at Trinity College, Cambridge. His rise thereafter was rapid: he became a Member of Parliament (MP) in 1589, then Speaker of the House in 1592. One year later, he was appointed Attorney General of England, edging out Sir Francis Bacon for the post. He gained added notoriety as a zealous prosecutor both of Sir Walter Raleigh and of the Gunpowder Plot conspirators. In 1606 he became Chief Justice of the Court of Common Pleas and Chief Justice of King's Bench in 1613.

Coke established landmark legal precedents protecting Britain's constitutional structure against attempted encroachments by the monarchy or Parliament. Perhaps best known is *Dr. Bonham's Case* of 1610, in which Coke found the Royal College of Physicians to have exceeded its constitutional authority in imprisoning Thomas Bonham for having allegedly practised medicine without a licence. Many scholars view the decision as an early expression of the doctrine of 'judicial review', where the judiciary retains jurisdiction to ascertain what limits the constitution may place not only upon executive, but even upon legislative authority (see page 36).

Certainly those lawyer-statesmen who founded the American republic, having split with Britain, saw things this way, and it was

Coke's interpretation of the constitution that the colonists accused the monarchy and Parliament of overstepping in the mid-eighteenth century. Moreover, the subsequent framers of the US Constitution, as well as the first US Supreme Court interpreters – notably John Marshall (see page 52) – considered themselves followers of Coke in their drafting and subsequent interpretation.

Coke's influence on common law stemmed from more than his judicial rulings, however. His two magisterial treatises, *The Reports* and *The Institutes*, were the principal sources from which American colonial and early republican lawyers learned the essentials of common law for many decades. The *Charter of the Virginia Company*, which Coke drafted, set an early precedent for written constitutionalism in the American colonies. Finally,

> 'Magna Carta is such a fellow, that he will have no sovereign.'
> Sir Edward Coke

Coke's *Petition of Right* formed the basis of the English Bill of Rights of 1689 and, through that document, also the Bill of Rights (see page 124), the UN *Universal Declaration of Human Rights* (see page 106), and countless other enumerations of basic human rights worldwide.

In view of Coke's role as protector of the constitution, even against the monarchy, it is not surprising that he occasionally found himself in 'hot water'. He was removed from the Chief Justiceship in 1616, whereupon he rejoined Parliament as an MP in 1620. There he offended the monarchy to such degree as to find himself imprisoned, with other Parliamentarians, for half a year. He returned the favour in 1628, leading Parliament in forcing Charles I to accede to the *Petition of Right* he had drafted – a development that contributed to limiting executive authority on a par with Magna Carta itself (see page 26).

Separation of Powers and Judicial Review

The notion of a constitutional separation of powers, policed by judicial review, is often associated, historically, with early modern British and American constitutional practice. But the idea is both much older than the British and US Constitutions and, by now, much more widespread than the Anglophone world. Moreover, through its association with related practices rooted in the ideal of the rule of law (see page 10), the kernel of the ideas of separation of powers and judicial review can be discerned far back indeed, in many civilizations worldwide.

At the core of judicial review is the idea of the rule of law, by which even the sovereign is subject to legal principles incumbent upon his, her, or its actions as upon those of anyone else. The practical question raised by this ideal is how, if at all, it is to be vindicated. Is the violator answerable to the Heavens alone, or should there be means of vindication on earth?

In many ancient societies, the question was, in effect, answered by respected clerics. Ecclesial or other personages viewed as interlocutors with the divine were often consulted by sovereigns with a view to the propriety of contemplated actions in light of heavenly ordinance. These same personages were often charged with the role of anointing, and in some cases even sanctioning, those with quotidian political authority. Many heated political controversies in ancient Greece, medieval Europe, and the Islamic world, to name three conspicuous examples, were indeed over the boundaries between ecclesial and secular political authority. And such controversies continue, of course, to arise around the world today.

But the idea of a separation of political powers, and enforceability of the boundary lines, ultimately came to be central even to questions of secular governance alone. In effect, the once solely ecclesial role of check upon executive (traditionally monarchical) authority came increasingly to be discharged first by legislatures – into which monarchs' advisors and peoples' petitioners evolved – then by judges – whose continuing practice of donning long gowns serves as a vestigial reminder of the ecclesial descent of their office.

Today's practices of the separation of powers and constitutional judicial review appear first to have emerged in their modern form in Britain. The first great theoretician of modern judicial review was probably Lord Coke (see page 34), though this is debated.

The talented generation of lawyers responsible for the founding of the American republic were much influenced both by Coke's writings, as well as by Montesquieu's interpretation of the British constitution (see page 44). The American founders, notably Jefferson, Hamilton and Madison (see pages 46, 48 and 50), designed what ultimately became the Constitution with Montesquieu's idealised interpretation of the British Constitution and Coke's writings very much in view.

From both the related British and American examples, the practice of separating core governmental functions and affording all persons a venue in which to vindicate the limits set upon each has spread worldwide. Most nation-states, indeed in form if not always in practice, now follow this pattern. It is the institutional counterpart to their societies' endorsement of the ideal of the rule of law.

Sir William Blackstone

Through his synthesis into one treatise of the diverse set of rules and principles scattered over the mass of judicial opinions constituting the common law of England, Sir William Blackstone performed a great service to the lawyers and citizens of his day. He also exercised a formative influence upon the legal understandings of generations of subsequent lawyers and judges in Britain, America, and indeed, all jurisdictions worldwide that are rooted in British common law.

Born: 1723, London, England
Importance: his *Commentaries on the Laws of England* formed most late-eighteenth-and early-nineteenth-century lawyers' understanding of the common law.
Died: 1780, Wallingford, England

Blackstone was born in London, in 1723, to a merchant family. He was educated first at the Charterhouse School, then at Pembroke College, Oxford. At Oxford he excelled as a student and was ultimately named Fellow of All Souls in 1743. Three years later he was called to the bar as lawyer at Middle Temple. Blackstone seems to have been better as a compiler and systematiser than as a practitioner of the law, however. He returned to Oxford for good in 1758, as Principal of New Inn Hall (subsequently to become St. Peter's College) and as first holder of what has since come to be known as the University's endowed Vinerian Professorship in Law. But Blackstone did not remain solely an academic, however. In 1761 he became MP for Hindon, and he also served for a time as King's Counsel.

Although he wrote treatises on Magna Carta (see page 26) and the British Charter of the Forests, it is primarily his *Commentaries on the Laws of England* (*Commentaries*) upon which Blackstone's reputation rests. Prior to Lord Blackstone, and especially prior to the time of Lord Coke (see page 34), the

English common law had been learnt principally through mastery of the vast body of case law, available only in written judicial opinions. There was little available in the way of systematic exposition of those basic principles and rules guiding those opinions and thus jointly underwriting the common law. Nor was there much in the way of attempts to glean conceptual continuities across areas of law. Blackstone's *Commentaries* changed all of that.

It is important to realise, in this context, that synthesis and systematisation of this sort are not mere 'abbreviating' or 'summarising'. They are also interpreting; and in that sense a well-conceived, well-exposited systematisation can affect all law and legal scholarship that follows – at least if read widely and admired by later generations of lawyers.

This is precisely what happened. For well over a century after publication, Blackstone's *Commentaries* were much read, admired, and followed by British lawyers and judges. In the US, the *Commentaries* were enormously influential for an even longer period. Indeed, to this day, American lawyers and judges cite them as definitive of how the common law would have been understood at the time of the American Founding. Abraham Lincoln and countless other distinguished lawyer-statesmen of the frontier period of American history first learned the law by reading Blackstone, whose treatise fitted comfortably in the circuit rider's saddlebag. So iconic has Blackstone been in American culture, in fact, that his *Commentaries* find mention even in, among other places, Herman Melville's *Moby Dick* and Harper Lee's celebrated novel of the heroic southern lawyer Atticus Finch, *To Kill a Mockingbird*.

Napoleon Bonaparte

Probably more books have been written about Napoleon than any other person from the nineteenth-century. His influence on early modern European history, including its legal history, would be difficult to overstate.

Napoleon was born on the Mediterranean island of Corsica in 1769, ceded to France by the Republic of Genoa one year before. In 1779, aged nine, Napoleon entered a French military academy near Troyes. Graduating in 1784, he next entered the elite Ecole Royale Militaire in Paris. On graduation in 1785, Napoleon took up duties as a second lieutenant in French garrisons at Valence and Auxonne.

It was with the outbreak of the French Revolution, in 1789, that his career began to flourish. In a number of military engagements, Napoleon, who sided with the Jacobins, proved a brilliant tactician against Royalists and then British, Italian and Austrian military forces. By the end of the eighteenth century he had won for France large portions of the Italian peninsula, Egypt and Palestine, the latter two wrested from the Ottoman Empire.

In late 1799, Napoleon returned to France from Egypt. The Directorate, which ruled the French Republic, had bankrupted the nation and earned a reputation for corruption and ineffectuality. Several Directors, including Talleyrand, sought Napoleon's support in a coup plot intended to place the Director Sieyes in control of the government. Napoleon obliged but successfully maneuvered to install himself instead, under the title of First Consul, established by a new constitution that he himself drafted. Two years later Napoleon secured ratification of yet another constitution, through which he became First Consul for life.

It was during the ensuing several years that he made his most lasting marks upon legal history. In addition to reforming the French systems of public finance, public transport, higher education and banking along lines that persist to this day, he instigated and presided over the drafting and promulgation of a number of carefully crafted legal codes. The best known of the Napoleonic codes is the *code civil*, drafted by committees of experts acting under Napoleon's ultimate authority, while Napoleon himself took active part in the final revisions. In addition to ending feudal systems of property rights, thereby expanding the rights of non-aristocrats to acquire and hold land, the *code* was pioneering in its rational summarising and ordering of the diffuse rules of contract and tort law that prevailed at the time. It also initiated an ongoing practice of regular codification of laws in much of Continental Europe and elsewhere (see page 19) and still serves as the kernel of many civil codes in Europe and beyond, including the state of Louisiana.

Napoleon's success in terms of law is twofold. Firstly, his codes spread to the many jurisdictions on Continental Europe that he conquered, where they continue to form the basis of much modern law. Secondly, he introduced partial administrative unifications of previously fragmented principalities in what have since become Germany and Italy. Those unifications are widely thought, in combination with German and Italian nationalist backlashes against French domination, to have prompted the eventual formation of the German and Italian nation-states.

Napoleon's military fortunes ultimately turned after the first decade of the nineteenth century. The battles of this period are the stuff of history, legend and art. He spent his last years in exile on the remote Atlantic island of St. Helena. He died at age 51, having come to count his *code civil* the greatest of his many triumphs.

Adversary Process and Inquisitorial Process

The distinction between so-called adversary and inquisitorial systems of justice-administration essentially rests on differences in the means used in assuring that relevant facts are ascertained, and justice is done, in adjudication.

As a historical matter, the distinction also relates to common law and civil law systems (see page 20), for common law systems have developed with adversarial proceedings, while civil law systems have done so with inquisitorial proceedings (the latter term deriving, in fact, from the same Roman law from which civil law derives). Conceptually, however, common law systems certainly could – and increasingly do – involve inquisitorial judges, while civil law systems for their part could – and to some extent nowadays do – include adversarial advocacy.

The principal difference between adversary and inquisitorial systems of judicial process, then, is in who takes initiative, and who bears costs, in trial proceedings. In the adversary system, it is primarily the parties themselves – plaintiffs and defendants – who develop arguments, seek evidence to support those arguments, and ask adjudicators to rule between them. In an inquisitorial system, by contrast, much of the initiative in investigating the circumstances giving rise to a legal conflict, and determining what the law has to say about the conflict, rests with the judge.

The inquisitorial system has the advantage of greater impartiality and objectivity, because one party's being more wealthy or clever than another seems less likely to bring an undue advantage at trial. The benefit of the adversary system, for its part, is thought to be a cost savings to the public fisc, in that the parties bear the costs of fact-discovery and argument-development themselves. Also, because the parties are personally interested, the adversary system is thought to produce the strongest and most zealous arguments possible on behalf of all sides.

As with the case of common law versus civil law legal systems, however, the distinction ought not to be overstated as a practical matter. While there was, in the past, a stark difference between the systems, in modern times each mode has come to incorporate elements of the other. Modern inquisitorial systems, for example, increasingly invite parties to introduce evidence and make arguments of their own to the court. Modern adversarial systems, for their part, have increasingly converted the judge presiding over trial from the earlier passive umpire role to a much more active, managerial role. Even 'umpire' judges now regularly meet with the parties to establish tight scheduling of all phases of trial, and police the now-fulsome 'discovery' regime by which parties afford one another notice of the evidence they have gathered and their strategy.

Judges in adversarial jurisdictions are also able to seek out information of their own that bears upon trial, through retention of court-appointed experts and even through on-site investigations of their own. In consequence, then, the adversarial versus inquisitorial distinction increasingly speaks more to historical and conceptual extremes than to hard-and-fast differences actually encountered in present-day legal systems.

Charles-Louis de Secondat, Baron de Montesquieu

Montesquieu was an influential French cultural and political thinker of the Enlightenment period. Though he is remembered for numerous intellectual contributions, it is his interpretation of what he took to be the British Constitution that was his most enduring influence.

Born: 1689, Bordeaux, France
Importance: his theorisation of the unwritten British Constitution proved influential upon later written constitutions worldwide.
Died: 1755, Paris, France

Montesquieu was born in Bordeaux in 1689. After studying at the Catholic College of Juilly, he married in 1715. This brought him a large dowry on the basis of which he could live the life of an independent scholar. The following year brought him yet more financial fortune when, upon the death of his uncle, he inherited both a large fortune and the Barony of Montesquieu.

These were heady times in European political history. Britain's Glorious Revolution had succeeded by the year of Montesquieu's birth, whereupon the nation had come openly to characterize itself as a constitutional monarchy. The year 1707 had brought England's union with Scotland. And 1715 saw the end of an era in France, with the death of the long-sitting and forceful Louis XIV. It was perhaps only natural that a young intellectual at the time of the French Enlightenment might come to reflect upon social and political developments of such magnitude.

Montesquieu quickly earned literary fame with his *Lettres Persanes* (*Persian Letters*) of 1721. The conceit was a fictional correspondence conducted by a Persian visiting Paris, through which vehicle he offered bitingly clever observations concerning the absurdities of modern French life. In 1734, he published an

Legislative

Executive

Judicial

influential work on the causes of the decline of the ancient Roman Republic. The work anticipated Edward Gibbon's magisterial *Decline and Fall of the Roman Empire* (1776) and also influenced subsequent generations of republicans, notably the American rebels of the later-eighteenth century, in their reflections upon the ever-present danger afflicting republics – that through political corruption they might degenerate into empires.

It is Montesquieu's anonymously published *De L'Esprit des Lois* (*The Spirit of the Laws*) of 1748, however, through which he has come to be both best known and most influential today. While its scope is much greater than a quick characterisation can convey, its careful attention to, and theorisation of, the unwritten British constitutional system, as involving a liberty-protective separation of powers proved enormously compelling to both British and British North American thinkers. In particular, James Madison (see page 50), sometimes called the 'father of the Constitution', greatly admired Montesquieu's work and cited it liberally when writing on behalf of ratification of new American law.

Montesquieu also proved influential on subsequent theorists and partisans of revolution in France and Continental Europe more broadly. Perhaps not surprisingly in view of his many interests, he travelled widely before his death, of a fever, in 1755.

Legal Innovators and Consolidators

Thomas Jefferson

Thomas Jefferson distinguished himself in youth as an intellectually curious young man. In later life, he did much to administer what became the US's first publicly funded institution of higher learning – the University of Virginia – and was an able and influential neoclassical architect. Jefferson's significance as a lawyer, however, runs paramount.

Born: 1743, Edge Hill, Virginia
Importance: author of American Declaration of Independence, Virginia Statute for Religious Freedom, and other influential legal documents and treatises.
Died: 1826, Charlottesville, Virginia

Jefferson was born into a successful tobacco planting family in the then-British colony of Virginia. Following his undergraduate years at the College of William and Mary in Williamsburg, Jefferson studied law and then joined the Virginia bar in 1767, handling hundreds of cases per year until 1773.

The deterioration of relations between London and its North American colonies in the early 1770s brought Jefferson into revolutionary politics. Having been elected to represent Albemarle County in the Virginia House of Burgesses in 1769, he landed at the centre of a budding rebellion. Following Parliament's passage of what came to be known as the Intolerable Acts, Jefferson penned a set of resolutions denouncing those enactments. These grew into Jefferson's *Summary View of the Rights of British North America*, which set forth a novel constitutional theory – one monarch, separate territorial legislatures – that ultimately came to pattern the British Commonwealth.

Upon the outbreak of open war between the North American colonies and Great Britain in 1775, Virginia sent Jefferson as delegate to the Second Continental Congress – the representative assembly that ultimately evolved into Congress. The Continental

Congress quickly began considering the prospect of formally declaring independence from Great Britain. It appointed Jefferson to the committee charged with preparing a document to this effect. He became principal drafter of what came to be known as the *Declaration of Independence*. The *Declaration* proved quite influential upon subsequent writing on political independence and basic human rights, including the *Universal Declaration of Human Rights* (see page 106).

During the revolutionary war years and after, Jefferson served in a number of government posts. He also exerted an important, if indirect, influence upon the new American Constitution being drafted in 1787.

From 1789 to 1793, he served as the first Secretary of State for the United States established under the new constitution, and began a bitter rivalry with Treasury Secretary Alexander Hamilton (see page 48). The pair were the principal advisors to President Washington, and each held radically divergent views of what manner of polity the new nation should become.

The divergence of vision between Hamilton and Jefferson broadly persists both in the dominant modes of constitutional interpretation in the US and in the counterpoised platforms of America's principal political parties – the Democrat and the Republican. Hamilton ultimately prevailed and in consequence, Jefferson resigned his position in 1793.

At the completion of Washington's second presidential term in 1796, Jefferson returned to politics to run for the top office. He narrowly lost to John Adams, Washington's vice president, and became vice president. By 1800, ironically with Hamilton's assistance, Jefferson became the US's third president.

After his years as president, Jefferson continued to write influential works. He died on July 4, 1826, fifty years to the day after the adoption of his *Declaration of Independence*.

Alexander Hamilton

Alexander Hamilton is best known as one of the principal authors of *The Federalist*, a brief on behalf of the then new, and not as yet ratified, American Constitution. Although *The Federalist* is justly celebrated as an innovative contribution to political theory, Hamilton's importance to the course of American law, politics and economy is much greater than this.

Born: 1757, Charles Town, Isle of Nevis, British Caribbean
Importance: Framer, defender, and theorist of Constitution; first US Secretary of Treasury
Died: 1804, New York City

Orphaned at the age of 11, Hamilton began working as clerk in the merchant house of one Nicolas Cruger and was soon running the business. By the age of 14, Hamilton had come to the attention of Hugh Knox, a minister recently posted to Nevis. Knox and Cruger arranged a collection to send Hamilton north for college-preparatory tutoring. Within months of his arrival, he had completed the ordinarily years-long course of study. He then gained admission to King's College (later Columbia University) of New York.

The American Revolution broke out during his time at King's and he soon enlisted in the Continental Army. His energy, tactical brilliance, organisational talents, and courage under fire caught the eye of George Washington, who asked Hamilton to serve as his *aide de camp*.

In the last years of the war, Hamilton was appointed New York Representative to the US Confederation Congress, with which he quickly grew frustrated for its ineffectuality in co-ordinating the war effort. In his spare time he drafted a resolution calling for the *Articles of Confederation* – the then Constitution – to be revised.

Hamilton resigned from the Congress after one year and taught himself law, swiftly gaining admission to the New York bar. There he earned renown both as a tireless advocate with a creative legal mind, and as an ardently principled defender of unpopular causes. He also founded the Bank of New York.

It was not long before Hamilton returned to politics in the newly independent republic. He served first as a Representative in the New York state legislature, then as a delegate to the Constitutional Convention in 1787. There, he collaborated with another brilliant young legislator, James Madison of Virginia (see page 50). The pair worked first in drafting and securing approval by the Convention of what became the Constitution, and then in securing the ratification of the constitution by the separate state legislatures. In this cause they cowrote *The Federalist* with John Jay, who became first Chief Justice of the US.

The new Constitution established, among other things, the office of the Presidency of the United States. Washington, first to fill the office, quickly named Hamilton his first Secretary of the Treasury. It was in this office that Hamilton, acting as virtual prime minister, made many of his most celebrated contributions to the new American polity's emerging legal and financial systems.

His contributions took the form, firstly, of numerous Treasury initiatives; and secondly, of memoranda submitted to President Washington and the Congress urging the constitutionality of those initiatives. Hamilton argued for a pragmatically expansive view of federal authority, which ultimately prevailed through its persuasiveness not only to Washington and most of the Congress, but also to the influential early Chief Justice John Marshall (see page 52). American constitutional lawyers still argue along 'conservative' Jeffersonian or 'liberal' Hamiltonian lines.

Though they continued to disagree upon many matters, Hamilton considered Jefferson a man of integrity. Jefferson reciprocated in his estimation of Hamilton, whom he counted as both sincere and ingenious.

James Madison

Like his colleagues Thomas Jefferson and Alexander Hamilton
(see pages 46 and 48), James Madison is one of those American
Founding Fathers who contributed much more to what became
the United States than can be easily captured in a few paragraphs.
His principal claims to importance, however, are in
connection with the US Constitution, one of the
world's first, written, nation-constitutive laws, and
the oldest such still in force.

Born: 1751, Port Conway,
Virginia
Importance: influential early
American legislator and
principal drafter of
Constitution.
Died: 1836, Montpelier,
Virginia

Madison was born in the Piedmont region of the then
British colony of Virginia, to a family of tobacco
planters. Often indebted to London financiers,
Madison, like Jefferson, appears to have felt a
lifelong antipathy to England. He attended the
College of New Jersey (now Princeton University)
from 1769 to 1771, completing its four-year course
of study in two years. He stayed on for postgraduate study
another year, for which reason he sometimes is called 'America's
first graduate student'.

Madison was elected to the newly self-declared independent
Virginia state legislature in 1776. There he quickly formed an
association with Thomas Jefferson, becoming something of a
protégée to his older colleague. During this time he assisted
with drafting Virginia's *Declaration of Religious Freedom*,
beginning a long history of work to keep church institutionally
distinct from state.

In 1780, Madison became a Virginia delegate to the rebellious
North American colonies' Continental Congress. There he began
his career as a legislator of renown, with both a mastery of
parliamentary mechanics and a prodigious capacity for crafting

and drafting enactments. With the coming of peace and national independence, in 1783, he grew increasingly concerned that the US government was too weak to effect the project of nation-building.

By the later 1780s, Madison had formed an alliance with Alexander Hamilton to draft and enact a new constitution. At the Constitutional Convention of 1787, held in Philadelphia, Pennsylvania, Madison's draft of the 'Virginia Plan' formed a basis for what became the US Constitution. Its three-branch federal system, comprising executive (president), legislature (congress), and judiciary (supreme court), was inspired in part by Montesquieu's interpretation of the unwritten British constitutional system (see page 44).

> 'The people have an indubitable, unalienable, and indefeasible right to reform or change their Government, whenever it be found adverse or inadequate to the purposes of its institution.'
>
> Bill of Rights, introduction

Madison was also largely responsible for drafting what became the first ten amendments to the new Constitution, known as the Bill of Rights. With Hamilton and, to a lesser extent, Federalist John Jay, Madison influentially advocated ratification of the new Constitution in the celebrated *The Federalist*. Madison's 'Federalist 10' is probably his most cited work today, forming the basis of much modern American theorising of political pluralism.

Madison remained active in his post-presidential years, continuing to advise US officials and even to legislate in Virginia well into his eighties. He died in 1836, at age 85, the last living signatory to the, now, well-established Constitution.

John Marshall

While the so-called Founding Fathers designed the US government on paper in the form of the US Constitution, John Marshall played a crucial role in determining the new government's actual functioning, as the new nation's most influential Chief Justice.

Born: 1755, Virginia
Importance: established pattern of effective judicial review by Supreme Court in the US, as well as US federal supremacy vis-à-vis the several states.
Died: 1835, Philadelphia, Pennsylvania

Marshall was born in the proverbial log cabin on the rural American frontier. His mother was a cousin to Thomas Jefferson (see page 46).

When the American Revolution broke out in 1775, Marshall joined a Virginia volunteer regiment and was soon appointed a lieutenant. He returned to the then capital of Virginia, Williamsburg, in 1779 to read law. He studied with George Wythe, a leading Virginia lawyer who had also trained Jefferson. Marshall briefly resumed military service in 1780 then, as the war began to wind down in 1781, he took up the practice of law.

In 1788, Marshall was named a delegate to the Virginia convention impaneled to decide upon ratification of the new US Constitution. Active in the new Federalist Party, which dominated American politics until the early nineteenth century, Marshall championed ratification. He continued his private law practice and served in a large number of government posts in rapid succession following the Constitution's ratification and the US government's taking on its present form.

It was as the fourth Chief Justice of the US, however, that Marshall made his lasting mark upon legal history. Taking office early in 1801, he brought vigor to a Supreme Court that had not yet begun to live up to its constitutional role as a third branch of

Above: As Chief Justice, John Marshall was responsible for establishing the Supreme Court as a centre of power and confirming the judiciary's position as an important, independent branch of the federal government.

government, co-equal with the president and congress.

Shortly after taking office, Marshall began a practice, which continues to this day, of announcing a single 'opinion of the court' rather than multiple opinions by each of the nine justices. He also, quite early on, penned what is probably the best known opinion of the Supreme Court: the *Marbury v. Madison* decision of 1803, which famously stated that 'it is emphatically the province and duty of the judicial department to say what the law is.' From that point forward, the practice of 'judicial review' (see page 36) after the manner of Britain's Lord Coke (see page 34) was firmly established in US constitutional practice.

Probably the other best-known decision penned by Marshall came in the *McCulloch v. Maryland* case of 1819, wherein the court both upheld the constitutionality of the Second Bank of the US and invalidated an attempt by the State of Maryland to tax that federal institution. The decision did much to ensure federal supremacy in the fledgling US constitutional system.

Marshall wrote many additional influential opinions for the court during this formative period. Perhaps fittingly, he was the US's longest serving Chief Justice, holding the office until his death in 1835. Having assumed the role when a strong central government and central court system were far from assured outcomes, he left a vigorous court and central government operating under the rule of law (see page 10).

Legal Innovators and Consolidators

Father of Commercial Law

William Murray, first Earl of Mansfield

Lord Mansfield's was a storied political and legal career. His present-day reputation rests principally, however, upon both his early judicial intervention in the cause of ending slavery in Britain and his laying much of the groundwork for modern commercial law in the Anglophone legal systems.

Born: 1705, Scone, Perthshire, Scotland
Importance: considered both the father of modern commercial law and a leader in the judicial abolition of slavery in Britain.
Died: 1793, Kenwood, London, England

Mansfield was born William Murray in Scotland, the youngest son of David Murray, fifth Viscount of Stormont. After graduating from Oxford University, he commenced legal study at Lincoln's Inn. He was called to the bar in 1730 and quickly made a name for himself as an effective and eloquent advocate in many high profile legal cases. He also came quickly to move among many of the most noted scholars and literary figures of his day.

Mansfield's legendary political career commenced with his election to Parliament for Boroughbridge and his appointment as Solicitor General, both in 1742. He became Attorney General in 1754, then Chief Judge of King's Bench in 1756. Even while on the bench, he was active and influential in parliamentary politics well into the 1780s.

Notwithstanding the many roles he played in British politics over the late-eighteenth century, it is for his judicial career that Mansfield is best known. Presiding over many important political trials, he is admired today for the impartiality with which he conducted them. What he is especially renowned for, however, is the role he played in the abolition of slavery in Britain and in the modernisation of mercantile law at a time when a busily commercialising UK and, subsequently, US, most needed it.

Mansfield's best-known contribution to the ending of slavery is his decision in *Somerset's Case*. James Somerset, legally counted a slave in the British colony of Virginia, was brought to England by his 'owner', one Stewart, in 1772. Somerset brought suit against Stewart, arguing slavery to be contrary to law.

Mansfield agreed with Somerset, famously writing that slavery was 'of such a nature' as to be 'incapable of being introduced for any reasons, moral or political.' He went on to say that nothing, in consequence, could support slavery but positive law, which he discounted as illegitimately 'preserv[ing] its force long after the reasons . . . from whence it was created [are] erased from memory.' In effect Mansfield held against positive-law-supported slavery on something approaching natural law grounds (see page 62), initiating a debate that led ultimately to the abolition of slavery by positive law itself.

A similar pattern characterises his contributions to commercial law. By Mansfield's day the medieval-rooted common law had come to prove sorely inadequate to the needs of developing commerce. Juries decided cases on the spur of the moment, with little to guide them, in turn leaving little if anything by way of generally applicable principles to guide later decisions.

Mansfield's impatience with outmoded and scarce-applicable precedent, as well as his knowledge of the more commercially sophisticated principles of Roman law (see Ulpian, page 32) and the streamlined customs of mercantile practice, served him well in his determination to bypass unhelpful common law precedents and develop a set of principles by which contract and related commercial cases could be rationally decided. The outcome was a fully developed system whose contours continue to guide most modern Anglophone contract and commercial law.

Benjamin N. Cardozo

Cardozo's influence upon the development of the American law of contract and tort can be likened to that of Lord Mansfield (see page 54) upon early modern British mercantile law. His influential judicial opinions figure abundantly in American law-school casebooks, and he is probably more quoted than any American judge other than Holmes (see page 82).

Born: 1870, New York City
Importance: influenced the law of contract and tort to a greater extent than any subsequent US judge has done.
Died: 1938, Washington, DC

Cardozo's father, Albert, was himself a judge, until implicated in a judicial corruption scandal during Benjamin's childhood. It is often suggested that a desire to restore the family name might have played some role both in Benjamin's hard work as a judge and in the notably elevated, moral tone characteristic of his written opinions.

Cardozo began undergraduate study at the age of 15, enrolling in Columbia University. Upon graduating he enrolled in the Columbia Law School in 1889. During his studies, Columbia lengthened the legal study program from two to three years; Cardozo declined to stay for the third year, so that, ironically, the US's most distinguished twentieth-century judge lacked a law degree.

Cardozo was called to the New York bar in 1891, and practiced in the city until 1914. Thereupon he became a judge on the New York Supreme Court – the state's trial court of general jurisdiction. Less than a month after taking this seat, however, Cardozo was appointed to the New York Court of Appeals –

'Danger invites rescue.'

Benjamin Cardozo, *Wagner v. International Railway*

the state's highest appellate body. It was here that Cardozo, over the ensuing 18 years, left his most profound influence upon modern law.

On the New York court, Cardozo developed the laws of contract, tort and product liability in ways that made more sense than received doctrine in a rapidly industrialising and nationally integrating economy. Modern promissory estoppel and third-party beneficiary doctrines in contract law, for example, were largely his development. Cardozo's development of proximate causation doctrine in tort law is likewise much celebrated. In enterprise organisational law, Cardozo's understanding of fiduciary duty doctrine is still regarded as the most morally exacting ever enunciated from the bench.

Fiduciary duty: A legal relationship of trust between two parties, namely a fiduciary, or trustee, and a principal, or beneficiary.

Nearly as noteworthy as the doctrinal innovation in Cardozo's opinions is the elegance of his writing style – not surprising, perhaps, in a cousin of the poet Emma Lazarus. The same style of exposition, and something of the style of thought behind his uniquely moral yet pragmatic approach to judging, is on display in Cardozo's still widely-read book titled *The Nature of the Judicial Process*, which is the published transcript of the Storrs Lectures he delivered at the Yale Law School in 1921.

It is hardly surprising, then, that Cardozo should have been named to the Supreme Court in 1932. The appointment was not only unanimously approved by the Senate and universally applauded by leading law faculties and legal personages across the country; it had even been called for by sitting members of the court itself, some of whom even offered to resign if necessary to open a place for him on the nation's highest court. It seems Cardozo had succeeded in restoring the family name.

Albert Venn Dicey

A. V. Dicey was an important latter-day exponent of the unwritten British Constitution, whose writings were so influential as today to be considered an integral part of that constitution itself.

Born: 1835, Leicestershire, England
Importance: influential theorist of British Constitution as guarantor of freedom and rule of law
Died: 1922, Oxford, England

Dicey was born shortly before the Victorian period near Lutterworth, in Leicestershire. In his late teens he attended Balliol College, Oxford, whence he took his bachelor's degree. Thereafter he read law in London and was called to the bar in 1863. After a successful practice he was named to the prestigious Vinerian Chair of English Law at Oxford, and Fellow of All Souls College, Oxford, in 1882. Toward the end of the century, he became one of the first professors of law at the new London School of Economics and served as Principal of Working Men's College, London, from 1899 to 1912.

Dicey wrote a number of highly influential monographs concerned with the British Constitution, constitutional theory and constitutional practice. He had a rich knowledge not only of British constitutional law and practice, but also of its American equivalent across the Atlantic.

That knowledge is on display in what is probably Dicey's most influential book, his *Lectures Introductory to the Study of the Law of the Constitution* (1885). Dicey argues therein, as well as in his monograph *The Privy Council* (1887), that the freedoms enjoyed by Britons are rooted both in the constitution-conferred sovereignty of Parliament and in the supremacy of the common law, as impartially administered by courts free of political influence. In this sense, he is a classic modern exponent of the

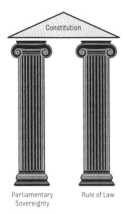

Left: Dicey argued that the British Constitution, supported by parliamentary sovereignty and the rule of law, was integral to protecting the freedom of British citizens.

rule of law, separation of powers and judicial review (see pages 10 and 36).

Dicey also warned that traditional British freedoms were imperiled by what he viewed as then contemporary encroachments upon those institutions. Perhaps in part for this reason, he remains much admired to this day by political and legal thinkers of a conservative or traditionalist leaning, both in the UK and in the US.

Dicey was a zealous opponent of Irish Home Rule, against which he wrote four books between 1886 and 1913, and about which he spoke often in public to the end of his life. He was, reputedly, much embittered by the formation of the Irish Free State in 1921.

Notwithstanding these facts, and his championing of parliamentary sovereignty, Dicey was also, curiously enough, an early supporter of referenda as a means of deciding political questions in the UK. Some of his thoughts in this connection can be found in his *Lectures on the Relation Between Law and Public Opinion in England* (1905).

Marcus Tullius Cicero

Cicero is one of the most celebrated lawyers, statesmen and political thinkers in history. His orations on behalf of legal clients, his legal and politico-philosophical writings, and his political career have been admired and cited for millennia.

Born: 106 BCE, Arpinium, near Rome
Importance: Roman statesman, lawyer and philosopher who infused Roman law with Greek philosophy and developed natural law and Republican political theory.
Died: 43 BCE, Formiae, near Rome

Cicero was born into a noble family in Arpinium, about 70 miles (110 km) from Rome and was tutored from an early age by his father, a knight. His abilities were prodigious and led to an invitation to learn Roman law from the distinguished jurist Quintus Mucius Scaevola.

Cicero was something of a polymath. In addition to learning the law inside and out at an early age, he excelled at poetry, history and rhetoric. By the time he had reached his mid teens, he is said to have 'fallen in love' with Greek literature and, above all, Greek philosophy. The influence is evident in his later speeches and more theoretical writings.

Cicero began his career as a lawyer about 83 BCE. Early on, he distinguished himself in his successful defence of Sextus Roscius, an enemy of the dictator, Sulla. Probably fearing for his life afterward, in 79 BCE Cicero departed Rome to live and study in Athens, still then the intellectual capital of Europe.

Cicero returned to Rome in the mid 70s BCE and commenced a distinguished political career, which included offices as Questor and Consul, among others. These were heady times in Rome, involving as they did social unrest, civil war, and frequent constitutional upheaval. Cicero was at times friendly with, and at times an adversary of, Caesar and Octavian, among other central figures of the day. He was often at the center of important trials

and high-stakes political struggles leading, ultimately, to his political murder in 43 BCE.

Notwithstanding the persuasive elegance of his many transcribed orations, Cicero has two principal legal legacies. Firstly, he systematically translated into Latin the Greek Stoical philosophy that he loved, with its attention to basic principles of justice among human

> 'The welfare of the people is the ultimate law.'
>
> Marcus Tullius Cicero,
> *de Legibus*

persons, thereby forging a Latin philosophical vocabulary. Because he drew most of his principles from this philosophy, moreover, he more or less single-handedly 'philosophised' Roman law, developing it into a body of practical justice doctrine that later developed into medieval natural law theory (see page 62).

Secondly, Cicero developed a rich theory of the Roman Republic and its basis in 'libertas', limited government, and a separation of powers among executive and legislature – an idealised, theoretic rendition of the practical constitutional arrangements that once had been in Rome and subsequently had been undone by civil war and dictatorship. In seeking to restore that ancient constitution, Cicero left an eloquent body of writings that both directly and indirectly influenced the North American and European political revolutions and written constitutions of the eighteenth, nineteenth and even twentieth centuries.

Natural Law and Legal Positivism

The question whether *lex iniustitia non est lex* – whether unjust 'law' really is law – is an ancient, if still a puzzling, one. Most people probably would not wish to dignify requirements imposed by armed gangs with the morally resonant term law'. Nor would they argue that anyone is morally obligated to obey any such putative 'laws'. Yet most people also would likely not wish to deny the term 'law' to any apparently bona fide legal provision, simply because they disagreed with it.

What, then, of statutes enacted by fascist legislatures or decisions rendered by corrupt judges or decrees issued by dictators against whom the citizenry cannot or will not rebel? When does that which behaves, at least superficially, like a government become, in reality, a mere gang? And when do coercively enforced decrees gain the full stature of 'laws' that one morally ought to obey?

These are among the most venerable questions of legal philosophy and disputes never have ceased in connection with them. Nor does dispute appear likely ever to do so, in view of the inherently porous and contestable nature of the concepts in question. But this does not mean we cannot usefully characterise well-known positions at the extremes of the divide and thereby possible middling positions between them.

'Natural law' positions lie at the *lex iniustitia non est lex* extreme of this divide. According to this view, if that which purports to be law is unjust, either because promulgated pursuant to unjust procedures or because substantively unjust in what it requires of citizens subject to it, it simply cannot be plausibly called 'law', nor is there moral obligation to obey it.

At the opposite end of this position is the pure 'legal positivist', who views laws as no more than the imperatival 'posits' of those with authority to rule. Of course, what counts as 'authority' – when such is legitimate and when it is no more than coercive capacity – can then become a difficult question in its own right. However, the hallmark of the legal positivist is that he or she holds that, so long as those latter questions *are* answered, what counts as 'law' follows straightforwardly: laws are rules authoritatively laid down by legitimate authorities, whatever the moral merits of the content or 'substance' of those rules.

Unavoidably, in view of space limitations, this distinction is a bit crude. There are very many subtly varying forms of modern natural law theory and legal positivism. Hardly anyone occupies either extreme position today. So-called inclusive legal positivists, for example, endorse the employment of moral principles by judges in interpreting legal provisions worded in moral terms (at least in legal systems that authorise this). So-called new natural law theorists, for their part, emphasise the role of moral principles more in the making of good law and the repealing of bad, than in whether to obey law on the books.

Increasingly, then, sophisticated legal positivists and natural lawyers today work out less extreme and more nuanced theories that attempt to do justice to our commonsense intuitions. There seems less disagreement over what is called 'law', which rules ought morally to be obeyed under what circumstances, and what role moral principles play in law's framing and interpretation. Such disagreement as is apt to remain seems increasingly rooted in questions of degree: namely, how wide or frequent the occasional gaps found between particular legal provisions or self-professed lawgivers on the one hand, and what justice counsels on the other, can grow before we no longer will call decrees 'laws' or be obliged to obey them until we are able to change them.

Jurists, Jurisprudes and Justice Thinkers

St. Thomas Aquinas

Thomas Aquinas figured so prominently in the intellectual life of the Middle Ages that it is difficult to contain him within only a few paragraphs. His principal siginificance to lawyers lies in his formulation of a comprehensive doctrine of natural law (see page 62), comprising a view of human nature, human agency, ethics, politics and law.

Born: *c.* 1225, Roccasecca, Sicily

Importance: great synthesist of Aristotelian philosophy with Christian theology and Roman law, deriving the most influential theory of natural law

Died: 1274, Fossa Nuova Abbey, Italy

Aquinas was born in his father's castle of Roccasecca in the kingdom of Sicily. His family was of noble lineage, his mother being related by blood to the Hohenstaufen dynasty of Holy Roman Emperors.

Because Aquinas's uncle Sinibald was Abbot of the Benedictine abbey at Montecasino, it was expected that Thomas would eventually enter the Benedictine order of monks and become himself an abbot. He began studies, aged 5, at a monastery near his home. Five years later he attended the University of Naples, where he completed studies aged 16. During his university years, Thomas decided to seek a vocation in the Dominican rather than the Benedictine Order. This displeased his family, who imprisoned him for a time in the hope of convincing him to abide by the original plan. Thomas held firm and, when Pope Innocent IV intervened on his behalf, took the Dominican habit aged 17.

Thomas showed considerable aptitude as a student and, in 1244, his Dominican superiors sent him to Cologne to study theology with the renowed Albertus Magnus. Within a year of Thomas's arrival there, Magnus was sent to the University of Paris, where Thomas accompanied him. Thomas earned his bachelor's in theology at Paris, in 1248, then returned to Cologne as a lecturer, returning to Paris in 1252 for his master's of theology. Thomas subsequently wrote and taught all over Europe, in such renowned universities of the day as those in Rome and Bologna in addition to Paris and Cologne. His greatest achievement during these years was his monumental *Summa Theologia*, a comprehensive work of theology, metaphysics and moral philosophy which synthesises Aristotelian learning with biblical and Christian doctrine.

Thomas's principal importance to lawyers comes through his account of natual law in the *Summa*. According to Thomas, human beings are endowed by God with a faculty of reason, through which they are able to discern the world as ordered and intelligible. Human beings, as creatures that are part of that world, flourish under some circumstances and do less well under others. They are in general, through the use of their reason, able to tell the two kinds of circumstance apart, and ethical and legal norms, in effect, register their determinations along these lines. Such is the case, in Thomas's view, irrespective of a person's religious beliefs, although faith comes naturally to those who see reason and intelligibility in the world.

These views met resistance at first from theologians of a more Augustinian disposition, who viewed God and God's commandments as beyond human comprehension and simply to be obeyed. In a sense, then, Thomas's opponents were early legal positivists (see page 62), focused upon sovereign will as *will* rather than *reason*. Thomas did not deny the importance of that will; he simply insisted that what God wills happens to *make sense* to us whom, after all, God willed also to create, and that laws made by more earthly sovereigns should be made to make sense – to be 'reason-able', one might say – as well. In so insisting, Thomas set the stage for such lawyers as Pufendorf, Dworkin, Finnis and Grotius (see pages 68, 96, 98 and 102).

Bartolus de Saxoferrato

Bartolus de Saxoferrato was probably the most influential interpreter of Roman law in the Middle Ages. Until modern times, most European law was rooted in, and developed from, Roman law doctrines. To be a scholar of Roman law during those times, therefore, was akin to being a scholar of the whole of one's legal system in any modern nation today. Bartolus's name featured in a common adage, heard around the late medieval and early modern times: *nemo bonus iurista nisi bartolista*. That is, 'no one can be a good jurist unless he or she be a Bartolist.'

Born: 1313, Venatura, Italy
Importance: most influential interpreter of Roman law in the Middle Ages
Died: 1357, Perugia, Italy

Bartolus was born in the Italian region of Marche. He entered the University of Perugia at a young age and read law under the renowned legal scholar, Cinus. Subsequently, he studied at the University of Bologna, which had pioneered the revival of Roman law scholarship centuries earlier and remained preeminent in the field. At Bologna, Bartolus studied under the great scholars, Belviso and Oldradus. He took his doctorate in law in 1334.

In 1339, Bartolus began teaching law in Pisa, moving shortly thereafter to teach at Perugia's law school. Within a short time, Perugia began to rival Bologna as a center of law study, thanks to the efforts of Bartolus. By 1348, Perugia had made Bartolus an honorary citizen in recognition of his work.

In 1355, the Holy Roman Emperor, Charles IV, appointed Bartolus his Consiliarius (counselor). Within two years, however, Bartolus died at the youthful age of 43. So renowned had he become in the Empire by then that a large monument was erected at the site of his grave in the Church of San Francisco. It was marked simply, in Italian, 'Bartolus's Grave'.

Notwithstanding the brevity of his life, Bartolus wrote many influential works of legal scholarship, both as professor and as counselor to the emperor. He penned important commentaries on all of the major divisions of Justinian's *Corpus Iuris Civilis* (see page 18). He wrote many treatises on specific legal subjects, perhaps the most famous being on riparian law (the law covering navigation and use of rivers). He also wrote hundreds of legal advisory opinions at the request of judges hearing legal cases, and in some cases at the request of prospective private litigants.

Bartolus was a great legal innovator. He derived numerous new fundamental legal concepts from his interpretation of Roman law, many of which remain in currency in civil law systems today (see page 20). The most enduring of these are in the areas of constitutional law – especially relations between larger political units like nations or empires and their smaller state or city subdivisions – and so-called conflicts of law (the set of doctrines concerned with how to resolve disputes between parties resident in different jurisdictions, which are subject to their own distinct, and conflicting, bodies of law).

Bartolus remained the most influential jurist in Europe well into the early modern era. His opinions were regarded as definitive in Continental jurisdictions for centuries after his death. Indeed some nations, such as Spain and Portugal, had statutes on the books to the effect that Bartolus's commentaries were to be treated as law wherever more immediate sources of law were silent. Such an image of the European legal scholar was Bartolus that both Mozart's *Marriage of Figaro* (1786) and Rossini's *Barber of Seville* (1816), featured pedantic lawyers named 'Bartolo'.

Samuel Pufendorf

Samuel Pufendorf is one of the critical transitional figures between medieval natural law theory (see page 62), modern natural law theory and the law of nations. His work was much cited and discussed by those eighteenth-century figures that led the revolutions in North America and France.

Born: 1632, Dorfchemnitz Stollberg, Duchy of Saxony
Importance: influential early-modern theorist of natural law and international law.
Died: 1694, Berlin, Prussia

Pufendorf's father was a Lutheran pastor, a vocation Pufendorf himself was intended to follow. After receiving his early education at the Fürstenschule at Grimma, he was accordingly sent to the University of Leipzig to study theology. He did not take to the subject, however, and took up public law instead.

Pufendorf then transferred to the University of Jena. There he soon found himself, under the influence of a mathematician friend, reading the works of Descartes, Hobbes and Grotius. Pufendorf completed his studies at Jena in 1658, earning a master's degree. He then took a position as tutor in the family of Petrus Julius Coyet, a minister of Sweden in the Danish city of Copenhagen. Coyet, before long, was caught up in political wrangles between Sweden and Denmark, and Pufendorf in consequence ended up imprisoned for a time with his patron. During this time he appears to have constructed, in his mind though not yet on paper, what he called a system of universal law inspired by his reading of Grotius (see page 102) and Hobbes. This he subsequently wrote and published, at the University of Leiden, in 1661, following his release from prison, under the title *Elementa Jurisprudentiae Universalis*.

Pufendorf's book was widely acclaimed. Perhaps partly in consequence of this, and partly because Pufendorf had dedicated the book to him, Charles Louis, Elector of Palatine, created a

chair at Heidelberg University for him. A sequence of celebrated works on jurisprudence, political theory and the proper relations between church and state followed, as well as sundry university posts and royal appointments throughout northern Europe.

Pufendorf is best known for his articulation of a set of basic principles of just relations among persons and states that amounts to a species of secularised natural law theory. In his rendering, the rights and obligations of human beings in relation to one another are not dependent upon the enactments of sovereigns, nor need they be viewed as having been promulgated by ecclesial authorities so much as they simply are inherent in human nature itself. Pufendorf took issue with Hobbes's view of the state of nature as one of continual 'warre' (conflict). Rather, he argued, the natural human condition is one of peaceful cooperation, but the state is prone to disruption by egoism and is, therefore, in need of buttressing by enacted and enforced law.

On the basis of his views of human nature and human relations, Pufendorf outlined principles that he argued were incumbent upon all persons irrespective of nationality, upon states in their dealings with one another, and even upon combatants at war. In this sense, he was a founder of modern just war theory as well as of international law and modern natural law theory.

Jeremy Bentham

It would be difficult to overstate the influence of Jeremy Bentham upon British, Commonwealth and, to a somewhat lesser extent, American law. His influence on Anglo-American economic thought and policy analysis might be even greater. This is not to endorse that influence, which has been controversial to say the least.

Born: 1748, London, England
Importance: early modern legal positivist, utilitarian and legal reformer.
Died: 1832, London, England

Bentham was born into a family at least two generations of which had included attorneys. He went up to Queen's College, Oxford, at the age of 12, earning a bachelor's degree in 1763 and a master's degree in 1766. Although he was called to the bar in 1769, he never practiced. He embarked, instead, upon a career as pamphleteer and legal reformer.

Bentham wrote prodigiously and on a variety of topics throughout his life, though most of his work was published posthumously. He thought the complex and incrementally growing nature of the British common law a scandal out of keeping with the rationalist spirit of those Enlightenment figures – Beccaria, Diderot, Voltaire and others – on whose writings he was educated. He advocated a thoroughgoing replacement both of the common law and of 'judge-made' common law methods of legal development more generally, by a neatly elaborated code.

Bentham viewed the endeavour to interpret law as giving expression to justice, reason or ethical principles to be illusory and pernicious. He argued that the law was, and should be, only that which the

'It is the greatest good to the greatest number 'of people which is the measure of right and wrong.'

Jeremy Bentham

sovereign legislated. He notoriously derided the concepts of natural law and human rights (see pages 62 and 124) as 'nonsense on stilts' and claimed that the only rights we possess are those conferred upon us by political authorities.

This view dovetailed with Bentham's pro-codification repudiation of judges' common law role as incremental discoverers of natural justice in deciding cases, and his concomitant advocacy that the law is to be fully elaborated in advance by the sovereign.

If the law is to be laid down in its entirety before the event (*ex ante*), and is not to be designed with a view to vindicating basic human rights, one might wonder what sorts of consideration are to determine a code's provisions. Here Bentham advocated what came to be known as his principle of utility, by which the law should be formulated with a view to 'the greatest good for the greatest number.'

When it was eventually brought to Bentham's attention that 'greatest good' and 'greatest number' could conflict, he abandoned the latter. Utilitarians have thus viewed policy and law as properly directed toward 'maximising' one or another quantum assumed to exist and be measurable – 'utility', 'welfare', 'wealth', and so forth. Critics ask whether such suggestions are any less nonsensical than that of basic human rights.

Bentham's thinking came to exercise a profound influence upon modern economic theorising and policy analysis. His influence upon law, in which human rights have steadily achieved wide recognition and practical vindication, has been rather less, however.

Utilitarianism:

Doctrine of seeking 'the greatest good for the greatest number.' 'Good' is here understood as hedonic utility – the presence of physical pleasure and absence of pain. As the two aims can come into conflict, modern followers of Bentham generally must choose either 'the greatest [aggregate] good', or 'the greatest number [of beneficiaries of policy]' as their principal aim.

Friedrich Carl von Savigny

Friedrich Carl von Savigny pioneered a distinctive approach to the study of law, known as the historical school, which insisted that the judge-developed law of a people must be systematically interpreted, explicated and appreciated as an expression of the fundamental values of that people before it could adequately be reformulated as a statutory code. This concept has constituted an important strand of legal scholarship ever since.

Born: 1779, Frankfurt am Main, German Principality of Hesse
Importance: principal founder and exponent of the influential 'historical school' of jurisprudence.
Died: 1861, Berlin, Prussia

Savigny entered Marburg University aged 16, and studied law under a number of distinguished German legal scholars. He also pursued studies at other German universities, including those at Jena and Leipzig, before returning to Marburg to earn his doctorate in law in 1800. His first book, published in 1803, was a learned treatise on the law of property from Roman times to the present. The book was an instant classic and quickly earned Savigny renown among European jurists.

In 1804, Savigny married Kunigunde Brentano, the sister of the well-known German writers Bettina von Arnim and Clemens Brentano. Savigny and Kunigunde traveled extensively through central Europe, during which time Savigny accumulated more and more knowledge of Roman law, which had been in force throughout Europe over the course of the Middle Ages.

In 1810, following a brief professorship in Roman law in Bavaria, Savigny took the Chair of Roman law at Berlin. Here, he founded what came to be called the *Spruch-Collegium*, a tribunal affiliated with the Berlin law faculty, that handed down advisory opinions on cases referred to it by ordinary courts.

In 1814, Savigny published an influential short work, *Vom*

Beruf unserer Zeit für Gesetzgebung und Rechtswissenschaft (*Of the Vocation of Our Age for Legislation and Jurisprudence*), in opposition to growing calls for a codification of German law (see Common Law and Civil Law, Custom and Code, page 20.) It was this work that proved influential in founding the historical school.

Savigny went on to produce a number of other significant publications including, in 1815, the *Zeitschrift für geschichtliche Rechtswissenschaft* (*Journal of Historical Jurisprudence*), an academic journal dedicated to work in the historicist vein that he had helped to pioneer, and the first volume of his magisterial *Geschichte des römischen Rechts im Mittelalter* (*History of Roman Law in the Middle Ages*), which illustrated how what had been a single European common law – the *ius commune* – split into distinct national legal systems. (The final volume of this influential work was not completed until 1831.) From 1840 to 1849, Savigny published the *System des heutigen römischen Rechts* (*System of Modern Roman Law*), an eight-volume work on Roman law as found in contemporary legal doctrine. Five volumes of collected shorter works were published in 1850 and an influential treatise on contract law was published in 1853.

Savigny's steadily growing reputation as a master of philosophic and historic jurisprudence brought him scores of academic awards and further judicial appointments. In 1842 he was appointed High Chancellor of Prussia. Upon his death, in 1861, legal scholars worldwide recognised that one of history's greatest legal scholars had passed. He had revived understanding of Roman law and its continued life in European legal doctrines. He had applied and reformed contemporary law in keeping with the spirit of Roman law as manifest in European law. And he had shown how fruitful legal scholarship could be when it combined accountability to historical fact with acute philosophic interpretation of the same.

Law and Social Science

Criticism levelled at the law by the legal realists (see page 80) has led to a substantial growth in studies concerning the interaction of law with other social phenomena. Of these schools of law and science, the best known is the law and economics movement.

The economic analysis of law, or 'law and economics', is an approach to the study of law, which emphasises the effects of differing rules and legal regimes upon wealth-creation. It bears both positive and normative faces.

The positive face of economic analysis of law suggests much common law legal doctrine exists due to judges' inarticulate intentions to develop rules that minimise waste and maximise value.

Positive economic analysis of law is often associated with the writings, during the 1970s, of then Professor, now Judge, Richard Posner. Few people seem to believe that this thesis can be seriously maintained any longer. Among those who largely repudiate positive law and economics now is Posner himself.

So-called normative economic analysis of law has proved longer-lived. The normative face of law and economics in effect simply replaces the 'is' of its positive cousin with an 'ought': adherents maintain that wealth-maximisation, even if it is *not* always the aim of judges and legislatures in crafting law, in all events *ought* to be. Wealth-maximisation, they maintain, is a good thing – better even than Bentham's 'utility' (see page 70).

Like its positive rendition, the normative face of economic analysis of law has been associated with the writings of Richard Posner. Since becoming a judge, however, Posner has grown more sensitive not only to the many more interests than aggregate wealth that the law actually serves, but also to the many more such interests that it properly ought to serve.

Particularly influential in the waning of normative economic analysis of law's influence have been the writings of Ronald Dworkin (see page 96) and formerly Professor, now US federal Judge Guido Calabresi. Both have emphasised the critical importance of distributional considerations in assessing the appropriateness of alternative rules and legal regimes. Other influential scholars, notably Jules Coleman at Yale, have noted that normative economics of law's conception of wealth is indeterminate.

Most American, and now many European, legal academies have at least some scholars who work within the law and economics tradition. But the tradition is broadening: there is now, for example, a growing school of so-called behavioural law and economics, which the influential legal academic Cass Sunstein has done much to popularise.

Many once-orthodox practitioners of economic analysis of law have, in recent years, moved in the behaviouralist direction. Many also have moved in the direction of so-called empirical legal studies, a family of legal scholarship long associated with Cornell Law School. Practitioners in this tradition seek to track, via sophisticated statistical methods of data-correlation, the effects of alternative legal arrangements. The effects in question can be not merely wealth effects, but any effects thought salient or interesting by scholars or lawmakers.

Empirical legal studies have spread throughout the legal academy worldwide in recent years. Many of its most widely read practitioners, moreover, are not only lawyers or economists, but also sociologists, political scientists and psychologists. In a sense, then, things have come full circle. For all of these developments stem from the approach to law taken by the realists, who for their part were regular interlocutors with that British school of legal thought known as sociological jurisprudence (see Holmes and Weber, pages 82 and 84).

Jurists, Jurisprudes and Justice Thinkers

John Austin

Working extensively in the philosophy of law and jurisprudence, John Austin was responsible for originating two interrelated strands of modern legal thought – analytic jurisprudence and legal positivism (see page 62).

Born: 1790, Suffolk, England
Importance: early developer of 'analytic' jurisprudence and legal positivism.
Died: 1859, London, England

Born to a merchant family in Suffolk, in early adulthood, Austin served in the British Army in Malta and Sicily but soon sold his officer's commission with a view to studying the law. He was called to the bar in 1818, where he practiced for seven years. Soon after leaving the bar, Austin was named the first Chair of Jurisprudence at what was to become University College in the new University of London. Bentham (see page 70) seems to have been instrumental in securing the position for him. From this position, Austin gave lecture courses over the years 1826 to 1832. Notes for one of these courses were published in 1832 under the title *The Province of Jurisprudence Determined* (*Province*), the book for which Austin is best known.

Austin's lectures seem not to have been well attended, and he resigned his Chair in 1835. A like pattern characterises Austin's brief time as lecturer at Inner Temple. Austin was subject to bouts of depression, debilitating self-criticism and, consequently, writer's block. His wife Sarah, a successful writer and translator, economically supported the family during their later years. She also worked tirelessly to secure Austin's reputation after his death.

Austin's reputation rests largely on two distinct strands of the theory propounded in *Province*. The first is the work's so-called analytic orientation. Both before Austin, and among many lawyers since, dominant approaches to legal theorising have treated the law as a cultural, sociological, political, economic and/or moral entity. Law is accordingly studied as a universally encountered feature of human life in community: a set of moral, cultural, political and economic institutions and norms, buttressed by courts in which rights and obligations can be vindicated, which help to order and improve social interactions. Austin, and the analytic style of jurisprudence that he pioneered, by contrast, focused upon law and legal methods in their own right and separate from their relations to other fields of study. The aim is to delineate the analytic relations among core legal concepts such as 'law', 'right', 'obligation', and so forth.

Austin seems to have been the first modern figure to study law solely in this fashion, and some modern jurisprudes have followed him in this course. The best known among them is Herbert Hart (see page 90).

The second strand of thought set forth in Austin's work is that of modern legal positivism (see page 62.) The essence of this doctrine is nicely captured in Austin's quip to the effect that 'the existence of law is one thing; its merit or demerit is another.' This view, though not identical with that of analytical jurisprudence, is nevertheless connected to it. The link is the treatment of law as autonomous – in this case, independent of moral inquiry.

At the heart of Austin's view are the theses that (a) law is a command issued by and forcibly backed up by a sovereign, while (b) the sovereign is simply him, her, them, or it, who is or are habitually obeyed. This 'top-down' view of law stood in some tension with traditional understandings of the British common law, according to which the law of the free Englishman, as *ratio scripta* (written reason), was justice itself as incrementally gleaned over time by wise judges endeavouring to settle disputes in principled fashion (see Common law and Natural law, pages 20 and 62).

Rudolf von Jhering

Rudolf von Jhering is sometimes said to have stood to the second half of the nineteenth century as Savigny (see page 72) stood to the first. The moral-philosophic approach to the interpretation of legal doctrine that he pioneered was set in deliberate opposition to Savigny's historical emphasis.

Born: 1818, Aurich, Hanover
Importance: founder of moral-philosophic school of European jurisprudence, in opposition to Savigny's historical school
Died: 1892, Göttingen, Prussia

Jhering began his studies at Heidelberg University in 1836, studying also in Göttingen, Munich and Berlin. Having received his doctorate in law in 1844, Jhering began teaching in Berlin, lecturing on what he called the 'spirit of Roman law'. He subsequently became professor of law, in rapid succession, at Basel (1845), Rostock (1846), Kiel (1849) and finally, for a sustained period of time, Giessen (1851).

Jhering came of age at a time when German jurisprudence was much under the influence of Savigny and his historical school. He set his own work in deliberate opposition to Savigny's historicism, labelling his own approach a form of 'natural jurisprudence', a modern, 'scientific' formulation of natural law theory (see entries on Natural Law and John Finnis, pages 62 and 98). On this conception, the law is a means of rendering a society more just.

The canonical expression of Jhering's jurisprudence is his landmark work, *Geist des römischen Rechts auf den verschiedenen Stufen seiner Entwicklung* (*The Spirit of Roman Law at Various Stages of its Development*), published from 1852 to 1865. It quickly placed him at the forefront of modern interpreters of the Roman law still influential in German legal doctrine. As with many German jurisprudes of the day, Jhering's account of Roman law was a typical means by which to advance views of the nature and functions of law more generally.

In 1868, Jhering accepted the Chair of Roman Law at the University of Vienna. His lectures there were attended by many Austrian cultural, scientific and political figures, as well as students. So renowned did they become that the Austro-Hungarian Emperor, Franz Joseph I, conferred a title of nobility upon Jhering in 1872.

One of Jhering's Vienna lectures, in particular, became renowned in its published form. This was his *Der Kampf ums Recht* (*Battle for Right*) of 1872. 12 separate editions were published within less than two years, and it has been translated into over 20 languages. Shortly after this work, Jhering published his almost equally renowned *Der Zweck im Recht* (*The Purpose of the Law*) in two volumes (1877 and 1883). In both works Jhering's arguments on behalf of justice and individual rights, the law's role in vindicating these, and the citizen's obligation to assert these was particularly forceful.

Shortly after receiving his title, Jhering returned to Göttingen, now as a professor. He seems to have preferred the relative tranquility of this ancient university town. He also took brief visiting professorships at Leipzig and Heidelberg during his later years as a legal academic.

It would be a mistake to say that Jhering was concerned only with obscure matters of high theory and fundamental rights. One of his most popular works was his *Jurisprudenz des täglichen Lebens* (*Jurisprudence of Quotidien Life*), published in 1870. Perhaps in keeping with this abiding interest in the ordinary, Jhering is said to have been an extraordinarily lively and friendly man, entertaining many a guest in his homes in each city he inhabited. He died in his beloved Göttingen, aged 74, in 1892.

Legal Formalism, Legal Realism and Critical Legal Studies

A venerable debate among legal theorists concerns the question as to what extent, if any, the law might plausibly be characterised as an autonomous intellectual endeavour, complete with its own axioms and methods of reasoning, such that outcomes of cases amount in effect to ineluctable theorems.

Those who have, historically, viewed the law as more or less autonomous in this way have, in effect, viewed the study of law as a 'pure' science and the deciding of cases as 'applied' science. In that sense, these thinkers have taken case outcomes to be, as it were, foreordained: given the law as it is, with its concepts and postulates, and given some fact pattern to which the law is applied, one can know in advance how a judge will decide, if correctly applying the law to the facts. Insofar as one takes this view, one is what classically has been called (often pejoratively) a legal formalist. The 'form' of the law decides the case.

Formalism of this sort has a history that dovetails with that of defenders of the 'letter' as distinguished from the 'spirit' of the law (see justice, law and equity, page 88). Indeed an entire school of ancient Chinese thought – that of the so-called legalists, inspired by the writings of the atheist aristocrat Han Fei and other champions of unrestricted state power – self-consciously defended strict letter jurisprudence with sophisticated, if individualism-indifferent, formalist arguments.

Just as adherence to the mere letter of the law finds detractors in those who champion the spirit of the law, however, so has legal formalism found influential detractors through history. The aforementioned Han Fei and his legalist school were influentially critiqued by Mozi and his followers, who viewed the true principle of statecraft as one of impartiality and fraternity in keeping with a universe animated by humanitarian concern – concerns in the light of which laws were to be interpreted. The best-known critics of formalism in modern times have been, firstly, those of the so-called legal realist and sociological jurisprudence movements of the 1920s, 1930s and 1940s and, subsequently, those of the critical legal studies (CLS) movement of the 1970s, 1980s and 1990s.

The principal efforts of the realists and sociologists centered on exposing a paradox in judicial decision-making. Notwithstanding their purporting to apply the same rules, maxims and forms of reasoning to legally similar fact situations, judges often reached contrary decisions, the realists observed. These are best explained by reference to legally irrelevant, yet politically salient, differences in the situations at hand. The outcome, these thinkers concluded, was that 'realistically' speaking, judicial decisions were 'result-driven'.

The realists and sociologists exercised significant influence on American and British legal thought through the twentieth century. Exponents of the CLS movement, in contrast, for the most part have not come to play a role on the bench or in government – though Roberto Unger of Harvard Law School, probably the most influential of the so-called crits and now a government minister in Brazil, is a notable exception. Possibly one reason for this is that, in contrast to the realists, the crits historically have concerned themselves less with how judges choose to interpret and apply inherently malleable legal doctrines in a manner subconsciously prompted by perceived, good-policy outcomes, than with how legal doctrines serve powerful social class interests.

Oliver Wendell Holmes Jr.

Asked to form a generic image of an American Supreme Court Justice, most people would probably envisage someone a lot like Oliver Wendell Holmes. His shock of white hair, ample moustache and oracular mode of speaking and writing all render him iconic. But his influence upon modern law has been much more substantial than that.

Born: 1841, Boston, Massachusetts

Importance: influential American judge and legal theorist

Died: 1935, Washington, DC

Holmes was born to a prominent Boston family in 1841. His father, O. W. Holmes Sr., was a well-known physician and writer, and his mother, Amelia Lee Jackson, was a near equally prominent abolitionist. The younger Holmes grew into an outspokenly opinionated adult often championing progressive political causes.

Holmes attended Harvard University, enlisting upon graduation to take part on the Union side in the Civil War. He is believed to have been much affected by what he saw during these years, remaining convinced ever after that governments and laws are rooted in violence. Certainly his later views upon law were in many ways positivist in orientation (see page 62).

After the war, Holmes returned to Harvard to study law and was called to the bar in 1866. He became a prominent Boston attorney, as well as a legal historian in his spare time. During these late Victorian years he spent much of his time in London, where he formed most of his closest friendships. He became one of the founders of what came to be known as the sociological school of jurisprudence in Britain, which would partly inspire the American school of legal realism (see page 80).

In 1881, Holmes published his influential treatise *The Common Law*, still widely read and discussed by legal scholars.

The book anticipates the realist school in its claims on behalf of pragmatic instrumentalism as the true basis of most judicial decisions. It also does so in its premise that that judges choose between competing legal rationales, in rationalising opinions, on the basis of 'inarticulate major premises' outside the law proper.

The year after *The Common Law* was published, Holmes was named both a professor of law at Harvard and a judge to the Supreme Judicial Court of Massachusetts. He distinguished himself in the latter post in developing a robust common law of free expression and a contract doctrine notable for its recognition of labour rights to bargain collectively.

In 1902, Holmes was named to the US Supreme Court. There he became known both as a champion of first Amendment free-speech rights and of the federal government's constitutional authority to regulate the economy. But Holmes was no unambiguous champion of natural justice or 'liberal lion'. His curmudgeonly denigration of natural law (see page 62) in the famous *Erie* case as 'a brooding omnipresence in the sky', and his willingness to uphold a Virginia compulsory sterilisation law ('. . . three generations of imbeciles is enough') in *Buck v. Bell* (1927) leave many believing that Holmes's Civil War experiences were not altogether salutary.

> 'We should be eternally vigilant against attempts to check the expression of opinions that we loathe.'
>
> Oliver Wendell Holmes Jr.

Nevertheless, Holmes's public lecture 'The Path of the Law', delivered during his later Supreme Court years, became a manifesto of sorts for the progressive legal realists of the 1920s. By the time he left the Court aged 90 in 1932, he had become not only the oldest sitting Justice in US history, but without doubt the most famous legal personage in the US as well.

Max Weber

Max Weber was not only a lawyer, but also one of the most influential and wide-ranging social theorists of all time. He is considered one of the founders of modern sociology, as well as of the study of the modern administrative state.

Born: 1864, Erfurt, Prussia
Significance: pioneered the study of law's interactions with social, cultural and economic factors – social theory.
Died: 1920, Munich, Germany

Weber was the eldest of seven children in a politically and culturally well-connected family. Many prominent figures were guests to the Webers' home. The young Max appears to have imbibed much of what transpired on these occasions, writing prodigiously on historical, philosophical and cultural subjects even as a child.

In 1882, Weber arrived at Heidelberg University to study law. He also took classes on theology, philosophy, history and economics. In 1884, he moved to the University of Berlin, by then a centre of European intellectual and cultural life. Weber continued his studies even while working as a barrister. By 1889, he had earned a law doctorate. By 1891, he had published his *Habilitationsschrift* – a German postdoctoral dissertation – and become qualified to hold a professorship in the German university system. At this time Weber also began to involve himself in German politics and economic policy.

In 1893, Weber married Marianne Schnitger, who later became a prominent feminist writer. The two moved to Freiburg the following year, where Weber took up a professorship in economics at Freiburg University. Two years later, he took up a similar position with Heidelberg University.

Weber wrote a great body of work during the 1890s, between bouts of severe depression that appear to have been catalysed by an unresolved quarrel with his father shortly before the latter's death in 1897.

At the turn of the century Weber resigned his university post, taking up an editorial position with a prominent journal, the *Archives for Social Science and Social Welfare*. In 1904, he published his best-known work, *The Protestant Ethic and the Spirit of Capitalism*. It established a now widely followed precedent in studying the role of religion and other cultural factors in the formation of legal and economic systems.

In the years immediately preceding World War I, Weber became involved in German politics again. During the war, he served on a number of German government commissions charged with planning for the postwar period.

During the immediate postwar years, Weber was involved both in the German negotiations leading to the Treaty of Versailles, and in designing the Weimar Constitution of postwar Germany. He also continued his studies and taught occasionally. And as ever, he continued to publish. In 1920, however, he contracted the Spanish flu and died of pneumonia as a result.

Many of Weber's most influential works were published posthumously. Among the many theories he developed is that of the modern state as an advance in the direction of what he called 'bureaucratic rationalisation', according to which, it is the hallmark of modern government that it acts increasingly through executive and administrative agencies staffed by experts and 'technocrats'. It has proved foundational for all modern accounts of administrative law and process.

Weber's combining of legal, economic, sociological and cultural factors in developing a comprehensive theory of society set the pattern for those interdisiplinary modes of legal study that have come to dominate legal academies worldwide since the mid-twentieth century.

Hans Kelsen

Hans Kelsen stands to modern Continental European jurisprudence, much as Herbert Hart (see page 90) does to modern Anglophone jurisprudence. Kelsen, however, has perhaps exercised more influence upon actual functioning institutions, including both constitutional courts and the United Nations, than any other philosopher of law.

Born: 1881, Prague, Austria-Hungary
Importance: influential European philosopher of law, who developed modern doctrines of legal positivism and constitutional review still in use by many Continental European courts.
Died: 1973, Berkeley, California

During World War I, Kelsen served as legal advisor to the Austro-Hungarian Minister of War. After the war he became, firstly, an associate professor in 1918, then a full professor in 1919, of public and administrative law at Vienna. There he taught a generation of subsequently influential legal theorists, founded and edited the influential *Journal of Public Law*, and helped to draft the new postwar Austrian Constitution in 1920. Austrian constitutional law continues to be based upon that founding document. Kelsen was subsequently appointed, in 1921, to a life term on the Austrian Constitutional Court.

Austria in the later 1920s saw the rise of right-wing political parties and militancy. Some decisions taken by the Constitutional Court attracted the ire of conservatives, leading to Kelsen's removal from the Court in 1930. Kelsen accordingly accepted an offered professorship at Cologne University, in Germany, where he began to concentrate his attentions upon positive international law. This posting did not last for long once the National Socialists took power in 1932.

Again removed by reactionary officials, Kelsen moved to Geneva in 1933 where, among other things, he wrote about and taught international law at the Graduate Institute of International

Studies until 1940. During these years he was also professor at the German University of Prague until the German annexation. At the beginning of this period, in 1934, Kelsen published his most influential treatise: *Pure Theory of Law*.

In 1940, Kelsen moved to the US, where he held a research associateship at Harvard Law School. That year he took up a visiting professorship in the politics department at the University of California at Berkeley. From 1945 on, Kelsen was a full professor at Berkeley until his retirement in 1952. During these years he published influential works on legal theory and international law. He also served as legal advisor to the United Nations War Crimes Commission in Washington, DC, assisting with preparations for the Nuremberg trials in 1945.

Kelsen's carefully rendered version of legal positivism (see page 62) has been particularly influential among modern legal philosophers. Central to his account is the concept of a *Grundnorm*, a fundamental principle upon which all features of a legal system are ultimately based.

In respect of constitutionalism, Kelsen's proposed model of review has proved decisive in Europe. According to this model, specialised constitutional courts are established to review legislation for its consistency with a polity's fundamental law. This is now the dominant model of constitutional review among most Continental European jurisdictions. In common law jurisdictions, by contrast, courts of general jurisdiction hear constitutional challenges just like any other legal claim.

In international law, Kelsen was responsible for much of the early conceptualisation of global institutions like the UN. He is, therefore, that relative rarity among lawyers who has sat as a judge, influenced the founding and shape of domestic and international institutions, and been recognised as a pre-eminent contributor to high theory in legal and political thought.

Justice, Law and Equity

A seemingly perennial problem afflicting legal systems is that of the occasional apparent divergence, in the context of particular legal cases or controversies, between the 'letter' and the perceived 'spirit' of the law.

Ideally, there is no such divergence: the law properly captures and gives adequate expression to that ideal, aim or purpose that has prompted the law's passage in the first place. Occasionally, however, either some infelicity in a statute's drafting, or some possible set of circumstances to which the provision in question appears to have application, but that was not foreseen by the provision's drafters, can result in a seemingly perverse outcome or unintended consequence. In many such cases, it is thought that those who vindicate the law – principally the courts – ought to vindicate the perceived spirit – the actual intent behind – rather than the mere letter of the law. When they do so, they do what in Anglo-American parlance is called 'equity'.

The *term* 'equity' derives from the idea of fairness, or natural justice. That concept's applicability here derives from the plausible presumption that the spirit or intent of the law is in general to do justice or, at any rate, not to work injustice.

The legal *institution* of equity descends from British practice. During the medieval period in particular, the common law vindicated at King's Bench was slow to evolve and less supple than it has since become (see page 20). Not surprisingly, cases of perceived divergence between the letter and spirit of the laws grew common. In such cases, petitioners often would seek the king's intervention. The king normally complied through his chancellor, who until comparatively modern times was a cleric educated in the traditions of Canon and Roman law. Canon and Roman law boasted robust doctrines of justice, which found expression in equitable doctrines, according to which Chancery would set aside certain judgments rendered by common law as unjust.

It is owing to this institutional divergence – that between King's Bench, which did common law, and Chancery, which did equity – that the distinction between letter and spirit of the law came to be described as that between law and equity. As it happens, however, Chancery's association with the monarch, or executive power, as distinguished from the judicial power sometimes evoked separation of powers suspicions (see page 36). Separate courts of equity were, in time, effectively folded into the same system of judicial administration as the common law courts.

Testamentary law:
Law concerning wills, trusts and inheritance.

The enduring legacy of equity, then, comes principally in two broad forms: firstly, the word 'equity' itself as a legal term meant to designate cases wherein courts apply legal provisions teleologically, with a view more to the provisions' perceived purposes than the strict letter of the language in which they are drafted, which over time can come to be misleading. And, more significantly, secondly, many doctrines and procedures originally developed in courts of equity, which continue to be influential in law courts today. Most of today's forms of court-afforded injunctive relief, for example, originate in equity jurisprudence, meaning that much of the law can be viewed as nothing less than court-enforceable justice.

Some US states continue to maintain separate equity courts or divisions within their judiciaries. Much of corporate law, family law, and testamentary law in the UK, US and other British-descended legal systems, moreover, derive from equity jurisprudence, while much of US procedural law is adapted from the streamlined judicial procedures developed in chancery courts.

Herbert Lionel Adolphus Hart

H. L. A. Hart is probably best known for harnessing the methods of 'ordinary language philosophy', prominent at Oxford in the 1950s and 1960s, to the task of revitalising legal positivism (see page 62) and the philosophy of law. But his contributions were broader than this.

Born: 1907, Cheltenham, England
Importance: introduced analytic jurisprudence in Anglophone world.
Died: 1992, Oxford, England

Hart was educated at New College, Oxford, before practicing as a barrister at Chancery from 1932 to 1940. He served in MI5 during World War II, thereafter taking a Fellowship in Philosophy at New College, Oxford. In 1952 he was elected Professor of Jurisprudence at Oxford, holding that Chair until 1969.

The title of Hart's best-known book, *The Concept of Law* (1961), self-consciously echoed that of Gilbert Ryle's *The Concept of Mind* (1949), an earlier canonical product of the Oxford 'ordinary language' tradition of philosophy – a school best known for its methodology. The guiding idea was that, to attain clarity on a subject of philosophical interest, one should first attend to how the principal terms of the field are employed in their 'natural habitats' of ordinary linguistic usage. In Hart's case, the terms included such words as 'law', 'rule', 'norm', 'obligation', and the like.

The outcome of Hart's efforts was a sophisticated version of an old idea: that of legal positivism. According to the earlier positivism of the English legal philosophers Jeremy Bentham and John Austin (see pages 70 and 76), law was simply the command of a habitually obeyed sovereign backed by the threat of force. By

Hart's day, the crudity of this vision of law had effectively discredited positivism as a viable legal philosophy in the Anglophone world.

Hart refined the positivist understanding of law in several critical respects. First, he attended to the great variety of ways in which legal norms actually came into being and were reinforced. Law's presence and operation, he showed, is much more pervasive and variegated than the old command theory had recognised. Hart came, ultimately, to label his empirically rich study of law's actual operations an exercise in 'descriptive sociology'.

A second way in which Hart refined positivist jurisprudence was by calling attention to a distinction between what he called 'primary' and 'secondary' rules. The former were rules governing conduct in civil society. The latter were rules governing the promulgation, amendment, and repeal of primary rules themselves. Well-developed legal systems, Hart maintained, always included both forms of rule.

Related to the idea of a secondary rule was Hart's idea of a 'rule of recognition' – a means by which citizens could ascertain what putative primary rules actually carried the force of law, and which norms did not. This idea fed into Hart's work on law's relation to other normative systems, in particular morals, which he took special care to distinguish from law even while acknowledging their cognate functions.

In this latter connection, Hart contributed more than a refined form of positivism. His work on the theory of criminal responsibility and theories of causation in the law, for example, were seminal. The end result of his impressive body of work was a much-revitalised Anglophone philosophy of law and legal subjects. And the debates that began in the 1960s between Hart on the one hand, and Fuller (see page 92) and Dworkin (see page 96) on the other, have continued among jurisprudes ever since.

Lon L. Fuller

Historically, if not substantively, Lon L. Fuller stands to contemporary natural law theory (see page 62) as Hart stands to contemporary legal positivism (see page 90 and 62). As professor and precursor to Ronald Dworkin (see page 96), moreover, his influence is still felt.

Born: 1902, Indianapolis, Indiana
Importance: instigated and decisively contributed to the development of contemporary natural law theory.
Died: 1978, Cambridge, Massachusetts

Fuller was professor of law at Harvard for decades, during which time he taught many who became influential legal academics in their own right. His contributions to the law of contract were significant as well. Without doubt, however, his most influential contributions to legal thought are *The Morality of Law* (1964) and his celebrated debate with Hart in the *Harvard Law Review*.

In the Anglo-American legal academy, natural law style approaches to law became outdated during the late-nineteenth and early-twentieth centuries. Indeed, philosophising about law had, itself, become rare in the Anglophone world. Hart's *Concept of Law* marked a turning point, both revitalising the philosophy of law and presenting a forceful restatement of the positivist approach to legal theorising. Fuller's *Morality of Law* was set in deliberate contraposition to Hart's great work, which preceded it by but a few years.

Fuller argued that putative legal provisions, to be recognisable as indeed legal, had to meet certain formal or procedural criteria, such as being mutually consistent and

'While perfection is an elusive goal, it is not hard to recognise blatant indecencies.'

Lon L. Fuller
The Morality of Law

prospective in effect. One way of viewing these criteria is as adumbrating a conception of the rule of law (see page 10). Because a legal system is critical in enabling people to plan their lives and live accordingly, Fuller argued, laying out the specific criteria that characterise it amounts to an explication of the internal, or formal, morality of law itself. Would-be legal provisions at variance with the criteria would, by definition, be incapable of functioning as law, hence of discharging law's role; they would also tend to be generally rejected by citizens as unfair.

Hebert Hart famously argued that Fuller confounded morality with efficacy, as even substantively repugnant laws – for example, the laws of National Socialist Germany – could constitute a system consistent with Fuller's criteria. Fuller had a rejoinder available to him, though he did not elaborate it as fully as he might have done. He noted that features that render a legal system efficacious do not for that fail to render it more moral as well. National Socialists would have been even more immoral than they already were had they promulgated and enforced pseudo-legal codes with retroactively applicable rules, individually naming the individuals subject to them, requiring what is impossible to perform, in language impossible for subjects to understand, and so forth.

Fuller might have generalised his rejoinder to Hart in this way: the possibility that laws might be substantively immoral, while procedurally fair, does not refute the claim that procedurally fair legal systems are moral in at least that minimal, procedural sense. Legal systems can be deeply immoral, hence subject to charges of one or another sort of invalidity, in more than one way. It was for Fuller's and Hart's shared student Dworkin, as well as later, new natural law theorists like Dworkin's and Hart's Oxford colleague John Finnis (see page 98), to explicate other such ways.

Political Philosopher

John Rawls

Though not, strictly speaking, a lawyer, John Rawls's towering stature as a political philosopher has led to the unusual distinction of his regular citation by courts of law and political figures throughout the Anglophone world and beyond.

Born: 1921, Baltimore, Maryland
Importance: probably the most influential justice theorist and political philosopher of the twentieth century.
Died: 2002, Lexington, Massachusetts

Rawls earned his bachelor's degree at Princeton University in 1943 and then enlisted in the US Army, as World War II was, by then, well underway. He witnessed firsthand the aftermath of the Hiroshima bombing in 1945 and is thought to have been much affected by what he saw. In 1946 he returned to Princeton to pursue doctoral studies in moral philosophy. He completed his doctoral work in 1950 and taught at Princeton until 1952, whereupon he took up studies at Christ Church College, Oxford University on a Fulbright Fellowship. There, he was apparently much influenced by Isaiah Berlin and Herbert Hart (see page 90).

Upon returning to the US, Rawls took up a position firstly as Assistant, then as Associate, and ultimately as Full Professor at Cornell University in Ithaca, New York. He then gained a tenured professorship at the Massachusetts Institute of Technology in Cambridge, Massachusetts, in 1962, followed two years later by another at Harvard University in the same city. Rawls taught there for most of the remaining 38 years of his life. He trained many who are now among the leading figures in contemporary legal, moral and political philosophy.

Rawls is best known for his monumental *A Theory of Justice* (1971), in which he revives a contractarian account of political and economic justice, as opposed to the utilitarianism that had, by then, been long dominant among Anglophone philosophers (see Jeremy Bentham, page 70). Key to Rawls's account is the methodological conceit of decision behind a 'veil of ignorance'. The idea is that impartial principles of social organisation are best viewed as those that would be selected by rational agents deliberating together before knowing what talents and handicaps they would labour under in the actual world.

Rawls famously argued that agents 'behind the veil' in his sense would settle upon two basic principles. The first is the priority of liberty, by which basic civil and political rights would not be traded off for material comforts. The second is the difference principle, by which departures from equality of material circumstance would likely be tolerated only to the degree that they resulted in bettering the material conditions of the worst off.

While many political thinkers since Rawls have questioned the particulars of his account of justice, all seem agreed that he revitalised the contractarian tradition and opened the field to the fundamental-rights-based conceptions of political justice that have since come to displace utilitarianism as a dominant approach to justice and political philosophy. His *Theory* remains central to the advocacy of basic human rights (see page 124) to this day.

Rawls has also been influential in other realms. His *Law of Peoples* (2000) is increasingly cited as a modest statement of global justice such as can gracefully be worked into international law. And his *Political Liberalism* (1993) is an influential statement of the doctrine of public reason.

Contractarian: A political theory that legitimate authority of government must derive from the consent of the governed, where the form and content of this consent derives from the idea of contract or mutual agreement. Also a moral theory that ethical norms derive their normative power from a hypothetical social contract, rather than from divine will or some other source.

Ronald M. Dworkin

Ronald Dworkin is one of the most influential living philosophers of law in the English-speaking world. He is also one of the most influential theorists of social justice since John Rawls (see page 94).

Born: 1931, Worcester, Massachusetts

Importance: has developed highly influential theories of a 'third-way' of law between positivism and natural law and resource-egalitarian distributive justice.

Dworkin briefly practiced law with the prestigious law firm of Sullivan & Cromwell in New York City, after which he began teaching at Yale in the US. In 1969, he was named Herbert Hart's (see page 90) successor to the Chair of Jurisprudence at Oxford. In the 1970s, he became, concurrently, Professor of Law and of Philosophy at New York University (NYU), positions he continues to hold. By the early 1980s he had become one of the most widely discussed political and legal philosophers in the world.

Dworkin has probably been most influential through his philosophy of law and his responsibility-sensitive, resource-egalitarian account of distributive justice.

Dworkin's account of law can be viewed as charting a third way between positivist and natural law accounts (see page 62). Legal positivists stress sovereign pedigree as the criterion for whether a putative norm counts as veritably binding law. Naturalists, by contrast, hold that the political-ethical legitimacy of the sovereign and, in many cases, even of that which the sovereign promulgates as law is critical in determining whether a dictate counts as a bona fide legal obligation. Dworkin's account is nuanced and difficult to pigeonhole but its fullest articulation is in his 1986 book, *Law's Empire*.

On the one hand, he treats a theory of law as a theory about how judges decide cases. They must make use of the precedent

Left: Traditionally, positivist law and natural law have been considered opposites, but Dworkin's work has charted a path between the two.

found in prior statutory enactments and court decisions. Those precedents can be called the 'posits' with which positivists are rightly concerned.

On the other hand, he argues, judges must *apply* the standards which legal posits are thought to embody. And applying a statutory provision or prior court decision is an inherently *interpretive* exercise. Given this, the question becomes: what constraints are to guide a judge's acts of interpretation?

Dworkin stresses two constraints. The first is the 'best moral interpretation' constraint. He observes that law is meant to achieve ends consistent with the good of a political community and its members, who count as moral equals. It is accordingly the judge's task to interpret particular legal provisions in keeping with the most compelling view of the good of such a community, which the provisions can plausibly be viewed as intended to further. In this sense, his account is naturalist.

On the other hand, he argues that *among* possible candidates for best moral interpretation, judges must select those that rest comfortably with *prior* decisions, which as noted before amount to 'posits'. In this sense, his account is positivist.

Dworkin's effort to walk the tightrope between positivism and naturalism is novel. Some remain unconvinced, but most seem to think that if he has not succeeded, no one can.

John Finnis

Today's rich revival of natural law theorising owes much to John Finnis. Almost all of the work carried out in this vein since 1980 amounts to elaboration upon his monumental *Natural Law and Natural Rights*, which has made Finnis one of the 'big four' in contemporary Anglo-American philosophy of law, along with Hart, Dworkin, and Raz (see pages 90, 96 and 100).

Born: 1940, Adelaide, Australia
Importance: initiated and significantly contributes to modern natural law theory.

Finnis was born and raised in Australia. He received his bachelor's degree in law at the University of Adelaide, where he won a Rhodes Scholarship. The latter took him to University College, Oxford, in 1962. There, Finnis earned his doctor of philosophy with a thesis on the concept of judicial authority. He has remained at Oxford ever since, where he is Fellow of and Professor of Law, respectively. Since 1995 he has also been Bolcioni Professor of Law at the University of Notre Dame.

Finnis grounds his account of legal phenomena in an account of the human good. In that sense he parts company with analytic jurisprudence of the Austinian variety (see page 76), even while employing the sophisticated methods of conceptual analysis characteristic of much modern Anglophone philosophy.

According to Finnis, there are basic 'goods' that each independently contributes to what he calls 'human flourishing'. These goods are incommensurable; one may not work against one of them even in the name of securing more of another. Our more general obligation as human beings is not to act contrary to what he calls 'integral human fulfillment' – the flourishing of all persons and communities of persons. Much of this foundational work is summarised in his *Fundamentals of Ethics* (1984).

Finnis's account of law and legal obligation grows out of his fundamental ethical conception. On this account the fundamental responsibility of any government is to further the aforementioned integral human fulfillment, and the law is to be regarded as an instrument in that endeavour. This places both formal and substantive constraints upon what counts as valid law. The formal constraints are those commonly figuring under the name 'rule of law' (see rule of law and Fuller, pages 10 and 92). The substantive constraints pertain to the *content* of putive legal rules, principles and other standards. Purportedly legal standards that are inconsistent with integral human fulfillment are fundamentally immoral, and in that sense not valid law.

Finnis does *not* claim that there is no obligation on the part of the citizen to comply with putatively legal provisions that *fail* the test of substantive morality. He distinguishes between the obligations of government officials in their governmental role, and the obligations of citizens qua citizens. There is no question that officials are obligated to amend or repeal invalid laws. The trickier question concerns citizens' obligations.

According to Finnis, in all but extreme circumstances. citizens are morally obligated to obey even such legal provisions as fail his substantive test for validity, for selective lawlessness weakens the legal system as a whole, and the rule of law is, itself, a necessary condition for human flourishing. The citizen's obligation in respect of substantively invalid legal provisions, then, is a counterpart to that of the government official: he or she is to work to see to it that such rules are repealed or amended.

In extreme situations' – where, say, government officials act systematically to harm those who are subject to them – *civil disobedience* rather than obedience may become morally obligatory. There can, of course, be circumstances in which it is difficult to decide whether the line has been crossed.

Joseph Raz

Joseph Raz is probably the most highly regarded exponent of legal positivism (see page 62) since his mentor, Herbert Hart (see page 90). He has also written widely, and again influentially, on a variety of subjects in legal, political and moral philosophy, including normativity, the theory of value, practical reason, and political authority.

Born: 1939, British Mandate of Palestine

Importance: most influential positivist philosopher of law in the Anglophone world since Herbert Hart

Raz was born in the then British Mandate of Palestine in 1939. He studied law and legal philosophy at the Hebrew University of Jerusalem, earning his Master of Jurisprudence degree in 1963. After meeting Hart at a conference in Israel, Raz traveled to Balliol College, Oxford to read philosophy under Herbert Hart's instruction. He earned his doctorate there in 1967 before returning to Hebrew University, where he served first as lecturer, then as senior lecturer.

In 1972, Raz was appointed Fellow and Tutor in Law at Balliol College, Oxford. He was subsequently named Professor of Philosophy of Law. Along with Dworkin (page 96), he has taught several generations of prominent legal, moral, and political philosophers.

Raz broadened the scope of Hart's sophisticated rendition of legal positivism by focusing not simply upon legal norms themselves, but upon the systems in which they are embedded. The relation to Hart's work is nicely brought out in the juxtaposition of titles of the two thinkers' best known monographs – Hart's *Concept of Law* on the one hand, Raz's *Concept of a Legal System* on the other.

Hart certainly did not concentrate upon particular legal rules to the exclusion of the legal systems in which they were at home, but his principal interest in legal systems was in respect of that

The law   Society

feature of developed systems whereby particular rules could be verified – 'recognised' – to be authoritative. Raz's focus has been broader in its concern with the full variety of features of a system of norms in virtue of which it can be viewed both as 'systematic' and indeed 'legal'.

Like other positivists, Raz has emphasised the conceptual distinctions between legal norms and moral norms. On his rendering, there is little conceptual interdependence between these phenomena. That is not to say, however, that there are no moral imperatives incumbent upon those who institute, maintain and work to improve legal systems. Indeed, his famed principles for the rule of law (see page 10) are to a considerable extent coextensive with those enunciated by Lon Fuller (see page 92) as constitutive of 'the *morality* of law'.

Raz's more recent writings have tended to focus less upon law and legal philosophy than upon practical reasoning, value, and normativity more generally considered. In his conceptual universe, law, morals and other kinds of norm are distinct, but nonetheless kindred, forms of practical action-guiding standard, each of which is best understood less in its kinship with the others than in its contrasts with them, and in connection with the system in which it is embedded.

Hugo Grotius

Huig de Groot, or 'Grotius', is widely regarded as having laid the conceptual foundations of modern international law, based upon an early modern natural law theory (see page 62). He was also, in his day, a highly regarded theologian, philosopher, poet and playwright.

Born: 1583, Delft, Dutch Republic
Importance: early modern natural law theorist, considered the father of international law.
Died: 1645, Rostock, Dutch Republic

Grotius was born during the Dutch revolt against Spain, the son of well-educated and eminent parents. His father began tutoring him in Aristotelian and humanist philosophy at an early age, and he attended the University of Leiden in 1594, at the age of 11. Leiden was, at the time, home to some of the most eminent scholars of Europe.

On graduating from Leiden, in 1598, Grotius began a life involving much travel through Europe, principally among diplomatic circles. He first went to France in the company of a renowned Dutch statesman, Johan van Oldenbarnevelt, on a diplomatic mission. There, Grotius is said to have much impressed the court of King Henry IV. He was also awarded an honorary Doctor of Laws degree by the University of Orleans during this time.

By 1599, still in his teens, Grotius was appointed an advocate at The Hague in 1599. Two years later, he was historiographer for the States of Holland. He became involved in matters of international law in 1604, when he was called to defend the Dutch seizure of a Portuguese vessel, the *Santa Catarina*, in the

> 'I saw in the whole Christian world a license of fighting at which even barbarous nations might blush'
>
> Hugo Grotius, 'Prolegomena'

Straight of Singapore during the Ibero-Dutch wars. Grotius eventually wrote his first treatise on the basis of this case.

After Grotius's first book, *De Indis*, there followed a prodigious torrent of writings, including *Mare Liberum* (*Free Seas*), in 1609, which brought controversy with British writers on the law of the sea at odds with Grotius. It was his *De Jure Belli ac Pacis* (*The Law of War and Peace*) of 1625, however, for which Grotius is best known by lawyers today. Shocked by the conduct of so-called civilized people during the Eighty Years War between Spain and the Netherlands, and during the Thirty Years War between Catholics and Protestants, Grotius sought some basis upon which to found legal rules of conduct that might govern parties in their decisions whether to go to war, and how to conduct themselves during war.

Grotius found the principles he sought in natural law theory, which he viewed as binding upon persons irrespective of their nationalities, and even irrespective of their divine ordinance. In his willingness to ground principles of natural justice in human nature itself, he set the pattern for all subsequent secular, natural law theorising. He also laid the foundations for modern international law, including the law of war and the law of the sea.

Grotius somehow managed to serve in a large number of lawyerly and diplomatic posts while writing his many treatises. Much of his time was spent in Sweden and in France. Perhaps, unsurprisingly, in a time of religious and political upheaval and war, he sometimes found himself in trouble with hostile political authorities. In his final years he was not permitted to set foot on his home soil – until 1645, when he died following a shipwreck that landed him at Rostock.

Dag Hammarskjöld and the United Nations

The Secretary General is the principal human face of the United Nations. Some have become major world figures but perhaps the most influential was Dag Hammarskjöld, who served from 1953 until his death in a suspicious plane crash while on a peace-making mission.

Born: 1905, Jönköping, Sweden
Importance: As second Secretary General of the UN, shaped the office's importance; helped resolve international disputes
Died: 1961, near Ndola, Northern Rhodesia (now Zambia)

The idea of a concert of nations to facilitate peaceful cooperation and a global rule of law is an old one. Various empires, both ancient and modern, professed aims to establish peaceful world order, and utopian-minded lawyers and philosophers proposed, and even drafted, detailed plans for voluntary such organisations.

It was not until the close of World War I, however, that serious efforts were made to form a *permanent global forum* for peaceful collective action by nations. The outcome of that effort was the League of Nations, founded in accordance with the Treaty of Versailles, in 1919.

The League did not survive the 1930s, however, as it failed to prevent the rise of the so-called Axis powers and their aggressions against neighbouring countries leading to World War II. It was during this conflict that the idea of a 'United Nations' gained global currency.

Winston Churchill and Franklin Roosevelt began to refer to the allied powers by this name in 1942. Wartime conferences hosted by these two leaders, along with those of the former USSR and the Republic of China, began expressly envisaging a formal postwar organisation of the same name. The culmination of these

United Nations Organisations

| General Assembly | Secretariat | Security Council |
| ECOSOC | Trusteeship Council | International Court |

Above: The pre-eminent body for global lawmaking and law enforcement, the UN's main organisations are the General Assembly, Secretariat, Security Council, Economic and Social Council (ECOSOC) and International Court of Justice (the Trusteeship Council was suspended in 1994).

developments was the United Nations Conference, held in San Francisco during April 1945, where the UN was founded.

The UN currently has over 192 members. Organisationally, it is divided over several distinct branches. The General Assembly, to which all member states belong, is the organisation's principal deliberative body. The Security Council is charged with deciding and acting upon matters of especial security importance. The Secretariat, headed by the Secretary General, serves as administrative corps for the organisation.

Dag Hammarskjöld was a prodigious student in his youth, and quickly became a distinguished lawyer and economist in his home country of Sweden during the 1930s, serving in many government posts. Upon assuming the Secretary Generalship of the UN in 1953, Hammarskjöld quickly transformed the office into its present form, energetically travelling the globe to defuse many developing wars and related Cold War crises.

Shortly before his death, Hammarskjold was nominated for the Nobel Peace Prize, which was awarded him posthumously in 1961. Upon his death, President Kennedy said, 'I realise now that in comparison to him, I am a small man. He was the greatest statesman of our century.' All of the best known Secretaries General since 1961 have effectively been walking a path cut by Hammarskjöld.

Founders of International Law

John Peters Humphrey

John Peters Humphrey was one of the most influential figures in the development of a robust regime of international human rights protection. He influenced not only the content of humanitarian law, but the institutional structures through which that law is vindicated.

Born: 1905, Hampton, New Brunswick, Canada
Importance: influential human rights lawyer who drafted, with Eleanor Roosevelt, the *Universal Declaration of Human Rights*
Died: 1995, Montreal, Quebec, Canada

Humphrey was born in Hampton, New Brunswick, in 1905. He attended the Rothesay Collegiate School, then the Mount Allison University in New Brunswick before moving on to earn his law degree at McGill in Montreal. He was called to the bar and began practicing law at the age of 24, in 1929. In 1936 he returned to McGill to teach on its Faculty of Law.

In 1946, the Human Rights Division of the new United Nations Secretariat (see page 104) appointed Humphrey its Director. In this capacity, Humphrey worked with Eleanor Roosevelt to draft what was to become the UN *Universal Declaration of Human Rights*. Roosevelt, who had been a vigorous advocate and prolific author on behalf of the poor and disadvantaged during the presidency of her husband, Franklin D. Roosevelt, was the first US Delegate to the UN, an institution she helped to found, from 1945 to 1952. The *Declaration*, which drew upon the English and the US Bills of Rights (see page 124; see also Constitutionalism, page 10, and Lord Coke, page 34), was adopted in December 1948 by a unanimous vote of the UN General Assembly. Roosevelt called it an 'international Magna Carta of all humankind' (see Magna Carta, page 26). She was herself called, by Humphrey and by President Truman, 'First Lady of the World' in virtue of her role in drafting and securing adoption of the *Declaration*.

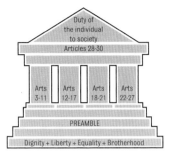

Though aspirational rather than literally stipulative of rights enforceable in international law, the declaration's enumerated rights, for the most part, were subsequently enacted in specific UN treaties with the force of law, in particular the International Covenant for Civil and Political Rights and the International Covenant for Economic, Social and Cultural Rights. Many of its provisions have also entered into customary international law.

Humphrey remained with the UN for 20 years. During this time he oversaw the implementation of scores of international human rights treaties, as well as of constitutions for newly independent states. In the early 1960s, he proposed that the UN establish a High Commisioner for Human Rights. This idea was put into effect during the 1990s, and the office has since evolved into that of a globally visible vindicator of basic human freedoms worldwide.

Humphrey returned to his teaching post at McGill University in 1966, but remained an active public servant both nationally and internationally for the remainder of his 90 years. He served on international commissions of inquiry into human rights offenses, and with numerous Canadian human rights organisations. He received the Order of Canada in 1974, and many human rights awards and endowed lectures are now named for him.

Rosalyn Higgins and the International Court of Justice

Born: 1937, London, England
Importance: First woman to be elected to the ICJ and its current president.

The International Court of Justice (ICJ) – also known as the World Court – adjudicates disputes between nation-states under international law. Renowned for the quality of its judges, Rosalyn Higgins was the first woman elected to the ICJ and has been its president since 2006.

Though the ICJ was founded along with the UN in San Francisco in 1945 (see page 104), it actually has a much longer lineage. It is the direct institutional successor to the Permanent Court of International Justice (PCIJ), established at the Hague, in the Netherlands, in 1922, as the judicial arm of the League of Nations.

In addition to adjudication, the ICJ also issues advisory opinions to the UN as to what international law prescribes in respect of particular questions submitted to it. Under its enabling statute, the court ascertains the content of international law by examining international treaties, international custom, general principles of law found to be operative in individual nations' domestic legal systems, and the writings of respected legal scholars (in that order). It has compulsory jurisdiction only over those nations that sign on to such arrangements by treaty. Nations that do not sign onto compulsory jurisdiction may, nonetheless, submit to jurisdiction on a case-by-case basis. The court comprises 15 judges, each elected to a nine-year term by the UN General Assembly and Security Council. They are selected from a list of candidates submitted by national groups in the Permanent Court of Arbitration, an international mediating institution founded in 1899 following the Hague Peace Conference. Elections to the court take place every three years, with one third of the judges accordingly replaced or re-elected on each such occasion, and the other two thirds remaining in order to ensure institutional continuity.

The ICJ is unique among courts worldwide for the quality of its judges, all of whom have earned renown as scholars of international law before their election to the bench. Exemplary in this connection is Rosalyn Higgins.

Higgins was born in London in 1937. She graduated from Girton College, Cambridge, with a bachelor of arts in 1959 and a bachelor of law in 1962. She pursued further study, earning the degree of Doctor of Juridical Science from Yale in the US in 1965. Following her education, Higgins became a London barrister and bencher of Inner Temple. She became a Queen's Counsel in 1986, and Dame Commander of the British Empire in 1995.

In addition to practising law, Higgins has taught in a number of universities and published many widely respected writings on international law. She was first elected to the ICJ in 1995 and has been awarded many honorary law degrees worldwide since then.

While the ICJ decided relatively few cases in its first decades, it has been frequently resorted to since the 1980s. Its decisions seem to be increasingly respected by most nations and its judges considered more prestigious worldwide. Indeed, thanks partly to the court itself, and partly to the growth of conferences and communications among high-court judges from around the world, we seem to be entering a world in which there can truly be said to be a global judiciary. This is thanks in no small part to the prestige brought to the global tribunals by the likes of Judge Higgins, as well as Judge Goldstone (see page 110).

Richard Goldstone and the International Criminal Court

Born: 1938, Johannesburg, South Africa

Importance: helped establish the first permanent international court in which individuals can be prosecuted for war crimes and other serious human-rights violations

The International Criminal Court (ICC) is a milestone in international law: the first case of a permanent international court in which individuals, rather than nation-states, can be parties. Success in finally establishing the court is no doubt attributable to several exemplary jurists who served on war crimes tribunals. Particularly important in this regard is Richard Goldstone, a world-renowned South African judge.

The ICC has precedent in a number of ad hoc tribunals established after armed conflicts for the trying of war crimes and related atrocities. But, until 2002, there was no continuously operating body in which institutional memory and expertise could be developed and whose presence might serve as an ongoing reminder to prospective rights-violators that they might be brought to justice.

The best-known precedents for the ICC are the Nuremberg and Tokyo Tribunals, held in 1948 after World War II. In the wake of those proceedings, the UN General Assembly determined the desirability of a permanent body that might exercise the same functions. It requested that the International Law Commission, established in 1948 with a view to 'promot[ing] . . . the progressive development of international law and its codification', draft a treaty that could serve as the legal foundation for such an institution. At least two such were drafted in the 1950s, but global political developments stalled any action being taken on them.

Further atrocities committed during the early 1990s in connection with wars in the former Yugoslavia and in Rwanda, along with the successes of ad hoc tribunals established to deal with such crimes, revived efforts to establish a permanent international criminal court. These efforts culminated in the UN General Assembly convening an international conference in Rome during the summer of 1998. The aim was to finalise approval of a treaty like that originally envisaged in 1948. The result was the Rome Statute of the International Criminal Court, adopted in July 1998. The statute came into force four years later, once 60 nations had formally ratified it in their domestic legislatures.

Richard Goldstone earned his law degree in 1962 and began practicing at the Johannesburg bar. By 1980 he had been named Chief Judge to the Transvaal Supreme Court. By the early 1990s he had become a Justice on the South Africa Supreme Court, charged with interpreting the new post-apartheid constitution and overseeing the transition to democracy.

Goldstone's distinction on the South African bench, and the quality of his opinions and writings, led to his appointment as Chief Prosecutor for the UN tribunals on Yugoslavia and Rwanda in the mid 1990s. The quality of his work there rendered the case for establishment of a permanent international criminal court all the more compelling. Goldstone now serves on many law faculties at universities worldwide, where he influentially lectures and publishes on the development of enforceable worldwide human rights law.

The ICC impaneled its first 18 judges in early 2003. It has already assumed a high profile in the global prosecution of human rights violations.

John Maynard Keynes and Bretton Woods

The Bretton Woods Institutions – the International Monetary Fund (IMF) and the World Bank – were born out of the desire to bring nations together to co-operate on economic arrangements following World War II. John Maynard Keynes, the best-known economist of the twentieth century, was influential in developing the institutions, along with his US counterpart Harry Dexter White.

Born: 1883, Cambridge, England
Importance: instrumental in establishing the principal organisations of gloal economic co-operation and integration.
Died: 1946, Tilton, East Sussex, England

A widespread perception toward the end of the war was that the global economic depression preceding the war had done much to cause it, and that the lack of international economic co-operation between nations had, for its part, caused the depression. It was accordingly agreed that, in addition to forming a United Nations organisation (see page 104), the nations that made up the postwar world should also forge a set of institutions that might facilitate closer economic integration. The Bretton Woods institutions were, along with the General Agreement in Tariffs and Trade (GATT), which evolved into the WTO (see page 114), the principal outcome.

Keynes had been retained by the British Treasury as a special advisor during the war. White, for his part, was a senior officer in the Department of Treasury. Both men were agreed that a regime of legally enforced stable exchange rates between national currencies would be essential in preventing a renewal of the competitive currency devaluations widely thought partly to blame for the global economic slump of the 1930s. Both men also agreed on the need for a global borrowing regime, to facilitate a stable currency regime and to enable war-torn economies to rebuild.

Keynes and White met repeatedly in the middle war years with a view to forging one set of institutions. At times these meetings grew contentious, but the two men and their negotiating teams managed to agree upon the basic contours of two institutions by 1944. The ensuing Bretton Woods Conference, in the New Hampshire resort town of that name, saw the formal founding of both institutions by a large group of nations.

The first was the IMF. As originally envisaged and operated, it served to administer a set of strict exchange rates between national currencies, all pegged to the dollar, which, in turn, was pegged to gold. That original 'par-value system' of strict currency exchange rates has long since faded, but the IMF endures.

'It has been our task to find a common measure, a common standard, a common rule acceptable to each and not irksome to any.'

John Maynard Keynes, Bretton Woods conference speech 1944

The second Bretton Woods institution – the International Bank for Reconstruction and Development, also known as the World Bank – was initially envisaged as a means of financing the reconstruction of war-torn Europe and Asia, but that role was quickly supplanted by bilateral aid arrangements. In consequence, it developed into an organisation to fund development projects in what has come to be known as the 'developing world'.

Both of the Bretton Woods institutions are affiliated with the UN. They also increasingly complement UN and related efforts to foster the development of democratic political institutions and robust domestic legal systems, which arguably are as critical to human development as roads, bridges and dams.

Yasuhei Taniguchi and the World Trade Organisation

The World Trade Organisation (WTO) is the principal organ charged with supervising and liberalising international trade. Yasuhei Taniguchi, who served the WTO from 2000 to 2007, is today revered as having set the bar for the quality of WTO decision-making.

Born: 1938, Tokyo, Japan
Importance: served and helped to establish the principal organ of global trade liberalisation enforced by law

As noted in connection with the Bretton Woods institutions (see page 112), destructive economic competition was viewed towards the end of World War II as having significantly contributed to the global depression preceding it. As the war drew to a close, world leaders accordingly sought to develop a set of liberal trade arrangements that would guarantee a brisk international commerce in goods and services. The result would be both greater prosperity and greater interdependence and integration among nations, which would help to maintain peace.

Substantive trading rules were successfully agreed in the General Agreement on Tariffs and Trade (GATT) in 1947. But the states involved were unable to agree on the shape and powers of an institution to administer the rules, and the ambition to establish such an organisation was tabled for nearly 50 years.

From 1947 until 1995, global trading arrangments were conducted in accordance with the GATT, which included several fundamental principles. These were designed gradually to reduce trade barriers and discrimination between member states' goods and services offered in a growing number of industries. Members also agreed regularly to meet, in the form of successive 'rounds', with a view to lowering barriers further, and to improving upon

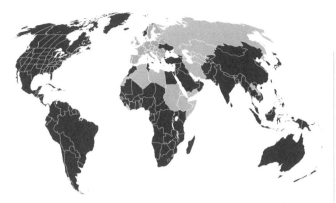

Above: The World Trade Organisation has 153 members (highlighted in dark purple). EU nations (grey) are members in their own rights, but are also represented as a whole, referred to as the European Communities.

means of administering and enforcing the rules.

The most momentous of these rounds was the Uruguay Round, held from 1986 to 1994 in Punta del Este, Uruguay. It was in this round that the ambition to establish an international trade organisation was finally realised in the WTO.

Through the WTO, member nations can challenge alleged discriminatory practices on the part of other members, through trial-like proceedings held before dispute panels. Panel decisions are widely respected, notwithstanding the controversy that often attends them. The principal reason is their high legal quality, itself a result of the high quality of WTO judges.

Taniguchi earned his first law degree from Kyoto University in 1957, and a JSD from Cornell University in New York in 1964. He has taught trade law and other subjects at many distinguished universities worldwide, including Kyoto, Tokyo, Cornell, Harvard and Stanford. Though retired, he continues to lecture worldwide. If the WTO proves ultimately as successful as it presently looks likely to do, it will be in no small measure owing to the pioneering work of Taniguchi and his colleagues.

Scipio Africanus Jones

Scipio Jones was an early champion of civil rights in the southern US, a region in which, during his life, such rights were hard fought and hard won. His ambition and self-taught legal mastery, by which he surmounted the poverty, lack of formal opportunity and racially oppressive environment from which he emerged, have inspired generations of lawyers since his own day.

Born: 1863, Smith Township, Arkansas
Importance: early civil rights champion in post-Civil War America.
Died: 1943, Little Rock, Arkansas

Jones was born to a former slave, Jemmima Jones, when she was 15 years of age. He attended segregated African American schools in his youth, then moved to Little Rock, the capital of his home state of Arkansas, in 1883. In Little Rock he attended Philander Smith College and then Bethel University, where he earned a bachelor's degree.

Jones then worked as a schoolteacher for several years after earning his bachelor's degree. In order to earn extra money, he took up work as a janitor in the chambers of several US federal judges in Little Rock. He began to read law books in his spare time during this period and before long was serving as an apprentice for, and reading law with, US Circuit Judge Robert J. Lea. Lea, impressed by Jones's abilities and determination, in effect served as his private law tutor.

By 1889, Jones had gained admittance to the American Bar Association. Shortly thereafter, he gained admittance to the Pulaski County (Little Rock) bar, entitling him to practice law.

> '(The Elaine 12 case is) the greatest case against peonage and mob law ever fought in the land.'
>
> Scipio Africanus Jones

He subsequently gained admittance to the Arkansas Supreme Court bar, as well as federal district, circuit, and ultimately the Supreme Court bars. He also started a number of successful local businesses in Little Rock.

As a lawyer, Jones took on many fellow African American clients, who tended not to be favoured by established white lawyers. He compiled a distinguished record of successful defences in criminal cases. Probably the best known of these was his defence of the so-called Elaine 12. These were 12 African-American sharecroppers sentenced to death by an all-white jury for their role in a 1919 race riot. Jones took the case all the way up to the Supreme Court, and his brief is said to have formed the core of the court's written opinion; he turned out to be, so to speak, a 'tenth Justice' in the case.

The court overturned the convictions of the 12 defendants on due-process grounds (see page 28), and charges were subsequently dropped against six of those 12 back in Arkansas. The other six were reconvicted to 12-year prison sentences, but Jones persuaded Arkansas's governor, Thomas McCrea, to pardon them. He also secured pardons for many others imprisoned by all-white juries for alleged crimes. This was no small feat given the time and place; indeed, it would be quite impressive even today.

By dint of his tireless efforts, great legal abilities, and force of intellect – all developed in the most hostile of environments – Jones remains a prototype for the hard-working civil-rights lawyer working against seemingly impossible odds. Well-known civil rights attorneys, such as Melvin Belli and Johnnie Cochran, have subsequently worked in his long shadow.

Clarence Darrow

Clarence Darrow is probably the most renowned trial lawyer in modern US history. Representing the least popular persons and causes, he nevertheless managed to win his cases on numerous occasions.

Born: 1857, Kinsman, Ohio
Importance: renowned attorney for unpopular causes.
Died: 1938, Chicago, Illinois

Darrow was born to activist parents. His father, Amirus, was an active abolitionist while his mother, Emily, was an equally active women's rights advocate and suffragist. Clarence seems to have imbibed the ethos of them both.

Darrow earned his bachelor's degree from Allegheny College, then his law degree from the University of Michigan Law School, both at a comparatively young age. He was admitted to the Ohio state bar at the age of 21, in 1878.

He first practiced law in Youngstown, Ohio, then moved to Chicago. He began as a 'railroad lawyer', working as corporate counsel for a large railroad company. He soon 'crossed the tracks', however, to represent labour unions and other unpopular clients in turn-of-the-century America.

Darrow's first high-profile client was Eugene Debs, leader of the American Railway Union in the infamous Pullman Strike of 1894. The same year, he represented Patrick Eugene Prendergast, who had confessed to the murder of Chicago's mayor, Carter Harrison. He mounted an insanity defence of Prendergast, which failed. It was the first, and only, murder defence mounted by Darrow that ended in the execution of his client. Darrow advocated passionately against capital punishment, which he considered barbarous.

Darrow's next renowned case was his defence of the

MacNamara brothers, who had been charged with bombing the *Los Angeles Times* building in a struggle to unionise the newspaper. He was able to plea-bargain reduced sentences for his clients in lieu of their being tried capitally. In another high-profile case, following the MacNamara prosecution, Darrow defended the infamous Leopold and Loeb, accused of murdering a teenager. Notwithstanding the notoriety of the crime, he managed to spare the defendants the death penalty.

After the Leopold and Loeb trial, Darrow began to take on causes of a more purely civil rights orientation. Many of his trials now involved African Americans accused of capital crimes. Even before all-white juries, he secured a surprising number of outright acquittals.

'We have the purpose of preventing bigots and ignoramuses from controlling the education of the United States.'
Clarence Darrow

Possibly Darrow's most famous trial was when he defended schoolteacher John T. Scopes, accused of teaching the theory of evolution in violation of Tennessee state law, in 1925. His principal opponent in the case was the renowned politician and former presidential candidate William Jennings Bryan. Their battle became the stuff of literature, drama and film.

Darrow's passion for unpopular causes, his politically progressive instincts and his eloquence rendered him legendary in his own time. He was a frequent invitee at public debates upon hot topics of the time – including one radio broadcast debate in New York with G. K. Chesterton. Since his death, in 1938, Darrow's reputation has only grown larger. He figures in more biographies, novels, plays and films, probably, than any other courtroom lawyer in American history.

Robert Jackson

Robert Jackson was the last member of the Supreme Court never to have graduated from a university. He is unusual in having served as a trial lawyer of sorts, even while a sitting Justice on a high court. It was in that latter capacity, however, that he made his biggest mark.

Born: 1892, Spring Creek Township, Pennsylvania
Importance: Supreme Court Justice who prosecuted Nazi war criminals at Nuremburg.
Died: 1954, Washington, DC

Jackson was born in rural Pennsylvania and raised in rural New York. He graduated from the Frewsberg, New York, secondary school in 1909, shortly thereafter beginning work as an apprentice in a Jamestown, New York, law office. He began attending classes at the Albany Law School, New York, and completed two years of study there. He then apprenticed for another year at the Jamestown law firm where he had begun, and gained admission to the New York bar, aged 21, in 1913.

Jackson began his own law practice in Jamestown, which proved very successful, and he earned considerable renown throughout New York as a trial lawyer over the ensuing 20 years. By 1934, his reputation had become national in scope. President Roosevelt, who had been Governor of New York, appointed him General Counsel in the Treasury office that later became the Internal Revenue Service, the principal federal taxing authority.

In rapid succession, Jackson next served as Assistant Attorney General, heading the Tax Division of the Department of Justice, Assistant Attorney General in charge of the Antitrust Division of the same department, and then Solicitor General of the US. Holding this position accordingly meant that Jackson was charged with defending the constitutionality of many of President Roosevelt's New Deal programs before the Supreme Court.

So effective was Jackson in this crucial role that Justice Louis Brandeis, a New Deal supporter on the Court, is reported to have said that Jackson should have held the position for life. President Roosevelt, however, had bigger plans for Jackson.

By 1940, Roosevelt had appointed Jackson as Attorney General of the US. One year later, he appointed him to the Supreme Court. During the ensuing 13 years, Jackson established a reputation as a great champion of individual liberties. He also came to be widely admired as a forceful judicial opponent of government overreaching. His eloquent opinions for the court are often quoted by American lawyers.

'That four great nations, flushed with victory and stung with injury stay the hand of vengeance and voluntarily submit their captive enemies to the judgment of the law is one of the most significant tributes that Power has ever paid to reason.'

Opening Statement,
The Nuremberg Trials

In 1945, Jackson took a leave of absence from the Supreme Court when President Truman appointed him chief US prosecutor for the Nazi war crimes trials held at Nuremburg. Jackson helped draft the London Charter of the International Military Tribunal, which governed the proceedings. He zealously prosecuted such top Nazi figures as Hermann Goering.

Jackson's arguments and cross-examinations during the Nuremberg proceedings have been depicted in drama and film. It does not seem a stretch to suggest that the trials, and Jackson's impassioned role therein, were influential on those who succeeded in finally instituting a permanent International Criminal Court in 2002 (see page 110).

Thurgood Marshall

Thurgood Marshall is probably best known as the first African American Justice on the Supreme Court. But his accomplishments in defending the constitutional rights of African Americans transformed American life well before his appointment to the court.

Born: 1908, Baltimore, Maryland
Importance: highly successful twentieth-century civil-rights lawyer and first African American member of the Supreme Court.
Died: 1993, Bethesda, Maryland, U.S.

Marshall was exposed to constitutional law comparatively early in life, as his father, William Marshall, was a vocal believer in both the rule of law and the Bill of Rights (see pages 10 and 124). Marshall was also, it seems, punished for misbehaviour as a child by being made to read the Constitution – a penalty, he reported later, that resulted in life-long devotion to the document.

Marshall attended Frederick Douglass High School, named for the famed abolitionist, in Baltimore. He graduated in 1926, thereupon attending Lincoln University in Pennsylvania, where he earned his bachelor's degree, in 1930. Marshall then sought to apply to the University of Maryland School of Law, but was told by the dean that his ethnicity would prevent his admission. In consequence, Marshall attended the law school of Howard University in Washington, DC.

Upon graduating from Howard in 1933 – the first in his class – Marshall began a private law practice in Baltimore. Within the year he had also begun working with the Baltimore branch of the renowned civil-rights organisation, the National Association for the Advancement of Colored People (NAACP). He won his first major lawsuit, in fornt of the Maryland Court of Appeals, two years later – satisfyingly, a suit on the part of an African American who wished to enroll in the University of Maryland School of Law.

Marshall's first case brought before the Supreme Court followed four years later. At the age of 32, Marshall won it. The same year he was named Chief Counsel for the NAACP. There followed a series of celebrated victories in suits Marshall brought on behalf of African Americans whose constitutional civil rights were violated by state action. Marshall won 29 of 32 suits argued before the Supreme Court. The best known of these was the landmark *Brown v. Board of Education* case of 1954, in which the court ended racial segregation of schools in America.

In 1961, President Kennedy appointed Marshall to the Court of Appeals for the Second Circuit, an influential American appellate court just below the Supreme Court. Marshall served on the court until 1965, when President Johnson appointed him Solicitor General of the US. In 1967, a vacancy opened on the Supreme Court, and Johnson appointed Marshall to fill it.

The first African American (and to date, one of only two) to sit on the court, Marshall compiled a distinguished record over the ensuing 24 years. With his friend and frequent ally, Justice William Brennan, he came to be known as a champion of constitutional liberties and equal protection of the laws. He was also a passionate opponent of capital punishment, dissenting with Brennan on every decision by the court that did not overturn capital sentences.

Marshall retired from the court in 1991 owing to failing health. He was awarded the Liberty Medal in 1992, and numerous public buildings and facilities are now named for him. He died in January 1993 and is interred in the Arlington National Cemetery in Virginia, alongside many other American civic heroes.

Natural Rights and Bills of Rights

The idea of natural rights, their enumeration in constitutional bills of rights, and their vindicability through due process of law are all closely linked to one another. They also are akin to the ideas of natural law and rule of law, as well as the practice of judicial review (see pages 62, 10, and 36). What distinguishes them from their kindred concepts and practices is their focus upon the individual citizen as beneficiary of the norms in question, rather than upon the government official as subject of the correlate duty in question.

The idea of a natural order of behaviour to which even sovereigns are subject is an ancient one found across cultures. Until comparatively modern times, however, the focus of this ancient form of normativity – that is, conforming to norms – was upon sovereigns and other governing personages. The principal vindicators of the norms, in turn, were either the deities themselves or their perceived representatives on earth, such as priests, prophets, or other ecclesiasts (see separation of powers and judicial review, page 36). Later – in thirteenth-century England, for example – the notion that such nonclerical figures as lords might also enforce law against a monarch gradually gained purchase. But still the idea remained that of one institution of governance – in this case the lords – enforcing its prerogatives against another – the monarch.

It appears not to have been until the seventeenth or eighteenth centuries that the idea of 'the people' as a whole – and then the individual citizen – as protector of their own prerogatives against government began to be systematically propounded by legal and political theorists. The idea came to figure prominently in the writings of early modern natural law theorists like Suarez, Pufendorf and Grotius (see pages 68 and 102). It also began to turn up in the 'social contract' line of political philosophers – in particular Hobbes, Locke and Rousseau. At first the idea took the form of a portrayal of constitutional arrangements as a kind of implicit agreement between ruler and ruled. Few suggested at this stage that the 'contract' might actually be enforced.

Modes of enforcement gradually developed, however, in the institution of judicial review – the same means by which the rule of law and the separation of powers are vindicated. Judicial review to vindicate natural rights as against governmental authority takes the form, in most modern legal systems, of recognised causes of action underwriting suits for injunction, or for damages (or both), which are brought by individuals or groups against legislation or executive action in courts. In most such cases, the mediating legal instruments are bills of rights, which themselves constitute portions of written constitutions.

The first modern written bill of rights appears to be the English one of 1689, which, although speaking to rights of individual citizens, treats the vindication of those rights as a matter of Parliament's contesting the claims of the Crown. The first bill of rights directed on behalf of the individual citizen appears to be that of the US. It was added in the form of the first ten amendments to the Constitution at the time of the latter's ratification by the individual states. The rights themselves were already well-established legal precedents of British common law.

Since the late eighteenth century, the idea of written bills of rights has spread worldwide. Most nations now have them, at least on paper, though actual vindicability in courts still varies. The *Universal Declaration of Human Rights* stems directly from this tradition (see page 106).

Renowned Trial Lawyers

Human Rights Campaigner

Clive Stafford Smith

Clive Stafford Smith is one of the most influential civil-rights lawyers practicing today. He is particularly well known for representing detainees at Guantanamo Bay in Cuba and for his campaigning work against the death penalty. He was awarded the Order of the British Empire in 2000 for 'humanitarian services in the legal field'.

Born: 1959, Cambridge, U.K.
Importance: influential civil-rights lawyer, opponent of capital punishment and defender of unpopular clients.

Stafford Smith was born in Cambridge, England, and educated first at Radley College. He was offered a place at Cambridge University but declined it to attend the University of North Carolina at Chapel Hill, to which he had won a Morehead Scholarship. At North Carolina, Stafford Smith studied journalism. He then attended Columbia Law School in New York City.

The early years of Stafford Smith's legal career were spent in the South, where civil-rights lawyers historically have been much needed. He worked for years with the renowned Southern Prisoners' Defense Committee, based in New Orleans, Louisiana. This was subsequently renamed the Southern Center for Human Rights, a name that means much to Americans concerned with civil rights in the South (see Scipio Africanus Jones, page 116).

It was during these years that Stafford Smith first came to public attention, in particular via Britain's BBC documentary *Fourteen Days in May*, which aired in 1987.

'In the US the law brings power to the powerless, no matter what a politician thinks the electorate wants to hear.'

Clive Stafford Smith,
Longford Lecture, 2006

This poignant work concerned the last weeks of the life of Stafford Smith's client Edward Earl Johnson, who was executed in Mississippi.

In 2004, Stafford Smith resumed residence in his country of birth, England. He is Legal Director for the UK branch of Reprieve, a human rights organisation. Probably his best-known clients of late have been Saddam Hussein, for whom Stafford Smith prepared a brief arguing for trial in the US under federal law in late 2004, and a large number of detainees held by the US military in Guantanamo Bay, Cuba. He recently published a book recounting his Guantanamo experience, called *Bad Men* (2007).

Stafford Smith's work on behalf of Guantanamo Bay detainees is widely viewed as being particularly heroic. His clients there – for the most part accused of terrorism – tend to be found unsympathetic characters. Stafford Smith would argue, however, that these are precisely the kinds of defendants most in need of protection.

What is more, many executive actions taken by the Bush adminstration, under which the Guantanamo Bay detainees are held, are widely viewed as running contrary to US constitutional rights provisions. Stafford Smith thus presents a most curious spectacle to conscientious Americans: one finds in him a British citizen doing more on behalf of US constitutional rights once asserted against British authority than most American lawyers themselves have yet bothered to do.

Notwithstanding his many accomplishments to date, Stafford Smith is still a comparatively young lawyer. There is much he is likely to achieve going forward. Citizens of the UK, the US and worldwide are likely to owe much to him by the time he has finished his legal career.

Index

For main entries see contents page. References to legal figures are given only where mentioned other than their main entry.